# Essays Connecting Spiritual Awakening & Animal Liberation

# Buddhism & Veganism

## Essays Connecting Spiritual Awakening & Animal Liberation

edited by Will Tuttle, Ph.D.

2018

Danvers

Vegan Publishers™

Vegan Publishers
Danvers, Massachusetts
www.veganpublishers.com

© 2018 by Will Tuttle, Ph.D.

Cover art by Madeleine Tuttle
Illustrations by Madeleine Tuttle
Design & typesetting by Nicola May Design

ISBN: 978-1-940184-49-4

# ◯ Table of Contents

## Vegan Perspectives from Primarily Theravada Contexts

## Vegan Perspectives from Primarily Vajrayana Contexts

# Honoring the One Body of Life

Joel & Michelle Levey

Can you imagine what it would be like to live in a world based on the principle of non-harming?

It's our pleasure and honor to offer this foreword to *Buddhism and Veganism*, joining the assembled authors of this brilliant, timely, and consciousness-raising book that invites readers to take a big step forward towards bringing this transformative vision of possibility to life in our world.

Albert Einstein reminds us, "A problem cannot be solved at the same level of thinking that created it... We shall require a substantially new manner of thinking if humankind is to survive." With every bite of food we eat, with every purchase of products we make, our wisdom eyes and hearts may be open or closed. In myriad moments each day, the impact of our intentions and choices ripple across the universe linking our lives with the lives of all beings. The Buddhist precepts, or "Mindfulness Precepts" as Zen Master Thich Nhat Hahn calls them, provide a profound and essential set of guidelines that support the flow of mindfulness into ways of living that are ever wiser and kinder.[1]

While many Buddhist teachers admit that it is impossible to practice the precepts perfectly, these guidelines function as a kind of spiritual North Star guiding our actions and intentions in the most liberating and beneficial direction for ourselves and others. As we practice them, our insight into our interdependence with all living beings naturally deepens and our compassionate concern expands. We become ever more care-full, or kindful, in finding a path through life that avoids directly or indirectly harming other living beings. While this can be a challenging, and even disturbing, aspiration to live with, when approached from a Dharma point of view, it can be a profoundly meaningful, effective, and liberating path toward awakening to our true nature and highest potential, and to helping others do the same.

In the *Mahaparinirvana Sutra*, expressing the Buddha's final teachings, the Awakened One spoke to Kasyapa, saying:

> "Blessed son, those who have the mindfulness of the *sravakas* [Buddhist disciples] are not allowed to eat meat from now on. Even if one is offered meat with genuine faith, one should see it as the flesh of one's own son.
>
> Bodhisattva Kasyapa asked Buddha, "Lord, why do you not allow the eating of meat?"
>
> Buddha replied, "Blessed son, eating meat hinders the development of compassion; therefore, all who follow the way of the Buddha should not eat meat from now on. Kasyapa, wherever a meat

eater lies, sits, or walks other sentient beings become fearful upon smelling him. Blessed son, just as when a man eats garlic others will keep away because of his bad smell, likewise, when animals smell the meat eater, they fear death..."

Kasyapa asked Buddha, "Lord, as monks, nuns and novice monks are dependent on other people for their food, what should they do when they are offered food with meat?"

Buddha replied to Kasyapa, "Separate the food and meat, wash the food, and then eat. You may use your begging bowl if it does not have the smell or taste of meat; otherwise you should wash the bowl. If the food has too much meat, one should not accept it. Do not eat food if you see that there is meat in it; if you do you will accumulate demerit. There will be no end if I speak thoroughly about the reasons I do not allow meat eating. I have given a brief reply because the time has come for my *parinirvana*."[2]

The universally respected 19th-century Tibetan master Patrul Rinpoche echoed this teaching for those following in the Buddha's footsteps, "As Buddhists we have taken the triple refuge [the Buddha, the Dharma and the Sangha]. To take refuge in the Dharma, one must practice non-violence to sentient beings. Thus, if we continue to eat meat—which has come from the slaughtering of innocent animals—then is this not a contradiction of our Buddhist commitments?"[3]

At the conclusion of his essay titled "On Meat Eating," the renowned contemporary lama Chatral Rinpoche wrote,

Knowing all of the faults of meat and alcohol, I have made a commitment to give them up in front of the great Bodhi tree in Bodhgaya with the Buddhas and Bodhisattvas of the ten directions as my witnesses. I have also declared this moral to all my monasteries. Therefore, anyone who listens to me is requested not to transgress this crucial aspect of Buddhist ethical conduct...

Those who argue that Buddha's condemnation of meat applies only to the seven classes of Theravadayana vows and is not related to the Mahayana and Vajrayana are clearly indicating their lack of proper knowledge. They have not seen the following Mahayana sutra passage: "Meat-eating is a diet that convolutes the three realms [of Samsara]. It is a sword that severs the potential for liberation. It is a fire that burns the seed of Buddhahood. It is a shaft of lightning that ends rebirth in the higher realms or a precious human rebirth."[4]

Many more renowned adepts have condemned meat as a poisonous food. Machig Labdron, a legendary female Buddhist practitioner, said, "For me, eating meat is out of the question. I feel great compassion when I see helpless animals looking up with fearful eyes."

We often say to our students that a good deal of courage is required if we are to take the wisdom teachings of the Buddhist tradition to heart, wake up to our lives and the world with mindfulness, and wholeheartedly practice the Dharma. When we open our wisdom eyes and behold the harsh, unwise, and misinformed happenings in the world, it can be devastating. It can be overwhelming to sit in the fires of bewilderment, rage, and the delusion of our separate self, or to conceive of the prevalence and magnitude of preventable suffering endured by human and non-human beings caused by humanity's ignorance, greed, and aggression. It requires courage and compassion to expand our circle of empathic awareness to resonate with the sufferings of countless animals who quiver in fear and pain. Upon contemplating the profound interdependence of all beings, we may come to the realization articulated by Shantideva when he exclaimed, "How wonderful it would be when all beings experience each other as limbs on the one body of life!"

It can be heartbreaking to comprehend the suffering of more than a trillion creatures each year whose lives are destroyed by industries that enslave, brutalize, and slaughter animals for food or animal experimentation. In addition, when we learn about the research indicating that our societal addictions to eating animal foods and using products derived from animals are destroying our environment and quality of life, it can be devastating. Further, realizing our own complicity in allowing this to continue can stir regret, shame, or denial. Although finding the courage within ourselves to dedicate our lives and practice to the personal and social justice engagement necessary to reduce this suffering can be daunting, such wholehearted compassionate action, based on the wisdom of interdependence, is also a path to liberation and full awakening.

As our wisdom eyes see deeper into the profound nature of interdependence through modern research, it is becoming increasingly clear that the current food production system is harming our lives and environment. The impacts of our current animal agriculture food production system are responsible for more than a quarter of all greenhouse gas emissions, more than all forms of transportation combined, eighty percent of which is associated with livestock production that utilizes nearly 66 percent of the arable land on earth to graze and grow feed for livestock. Unhealthy diets and high body weight are among the greatest contributors to premature mortality worldwide. Transitioning toward a plant-based diet, in line with standard dietary guidelines, could reduce global mortality by six to ten percent and food-related greenhouse gas emissions by 29 to 70 percent.[5]

In his seminal book, *To Cherish All Life,* Roshi Philip Kapleau emphasizes the dignity and innate holiness of animals and their basic kinship with humanity. He reflects,

> In Buddhism the first precept of not killing, or harmlessness, is grounded in our Buddha-nature — the matrix of all phenomena — from which arises our sense of compassion and moral goodness...It is in Buddha-nature that all existences are unified and harmonized. To willfully take life means to disrupt and destroy this inherent wholeness and to blunt feelings of reverence and compassion arising from our Buddha-mind. The first precept of not killing is really a call to life and creation even as it is a condemnation of death and destruction.[6]

Central to the compassionate practices of Buddhism is the practice of the Four Immeasurables. One of the most inspiring traditional versions of this practice and prayer is when we take it upon ourselves to create the causes and conditions for these qualities to flourish in our lives and world:

> If all beings had happiness and the causes of happiness, how wonderful it would be! May they come to have these. I will cause them to have these...
> If all beings were free from suffering and the causes of suffering, how wonderful it would be! May they come to be free from these. I will cause them to be free from these...
> If all beings did not lack the immeasurable joy of liberation, how wonderful it would be! May they come not to lack this. I will cause them not to lack this...

And, if all beings were to abide in immeasurable equanimity, free from attachment and hatred, how wonderful it would be! May they come to abide so. I will cause them to abide so...

I pray for empowerment from all the great teachers and wisdom beings to enable me to do this.

Just as Dharma practice requires deep care, study, and discipline to awaken, not just for our own well-being but to benefit and liberate all beings, so too, making the transition to a non-harming, plant-based vegan lifestyle requires the study and discipline, courage and care necessary to go beyond the familiar customs, habits, identities, and lifestyles in which we have previously taken refuge and around which we have formed our identity. As our Dharma practice deepens and matures, we will naturally gravitate toward making choices that reflect deeper wisdom and loving kindness.

When told by a farmer that we humans need to eat meat to get the stuff that bones are made of (read 'protein'), Henry David Thoreau pointed out that the farmer and his plow are being pulled behind a husky team of oxen and skillfully wondered why the farmer doesn't see that the much more powerful bones and muscles of the oxen are built solely by plants. Having lived as healthy, vibrant, Dharma practitioners and vegetarians for fifty years, and vegans for thirty-plus years, we can say from our experience that there has never been a time in our lives when shifting to a plant-based lifestyle is easier, more well-informed and resourced, when there are so many healthy and delicious options available, and when it is so clearly essential in terms of social and environmental justice.

We encourage you to read this profound and inspiring collection of teachings on veganism and Buddhism as a meditation. Be mindful of how the words and stories offered here touch you, resonate with your own deep intuitive wisdom and noble true heart, and nudge, if not catapult, you toward living with an ever-deepening commitment to making choices that propel you into being a force for the good of all.

*"A human being is part of the whole called by us the Universe.*
*We experience ourselves, our thoughts and feelings*
*as something separated from the rest,*
*a kind of optical delusion of consciousness.*
*This delusion is a kind of prison for us,*
*restricting us to our personal desires*
*and to affection for a few persons nearest us.*
*Our task must be to free ourselves from this prison*
*by widening our circle of compassion to embrace all living creatures,*
*and the whole of nature in all of its beauty.*
*Nobody is able to achieve this completely,*
*but striving for such achievement is, in itself, a part of the liberation*
*and foundation for inner security."*
~ Albert Einstein

May all beings widen the circle of their compassion to be free, be happy, be safe, be at ease, and awaken to their true nature and highest potentials.

References:
1.  Hanh, Thich Nhat. *For a Future to be Possible: Buddhist Ethics for Daily Life*, Parallax Press, 1993.
2.  *Mahaparinirvana Sutra*, tr. Kosho Yamamoto, The Karinbunko, p. 91. *Parinirvana* refers to the Buddha's physical passing from the human realm into the state of enlightenment.
3.  Cited in Chatral Rinpoche, *Compassionate Action: The Teachings of Chatral Rinpoche*, Zach Larson (ed.), Snow Lion, 2007. Chapter 3.
4.  Chatral Rinpoche, *op. cit.*
5.  Springmann, M., et al. "Analysis and valuation of the health and climate change co-benefits of dietary change." *Proceedings of the National Academy of Sciences*, Marco Springmann, 4146–4151
6.  Kapleau, Roshi Philip, *To Cherish All Life: A Buddhist Case for Becoming Vegetarian*, 1986.

# Do Buddhist Teachings Mandate Veganism?

Will Tuttle

Many of us are surprised to discover that Buddhist monks, lamas, and teachers often eat meat. This may be contrary to our image of the disciplined and compassionate lifestyle we expect such people to exemplify. As several essays in this book explain, the Theravada and Tibetan Buddhist traditions typically allow eating animal-sourced foods, while the Mahayana traditions have tended to make vegan living an integral part of their teachings. Additionally, as the more heavily meat and dairy consuming Western culture has impacted all these traditions over the past several centuries, and as these traditions bring their teachings to the West, they have understandably been influenced by Western culture and have moved away from earlier, more vegan orientations.

So, what is the underlying relationship between Buddhism and veganism? Do the Buddhist teachings require or explicitly encourage vegan living, or is veganism seen as a mere personal choice? As Buddhism continues to spread, and as interest in veganism is burgeoning, these questions are heating up, and deserve a more thorough investigation and understanding. This book is a collection of essays by people who are committed to both Buddhism and veganism, and who share a variety of perspectives on how these two practices deepen and reinforce each other.

All Buddhist traditions honor the foundational teaching of the Five Precepts (refraining from killing, stealing, deceiving, sexual misconduct, and using, or causing others to use, toxic drugs), which is similar to veganism regarding our treatment of animals. A second fundamental Buddhist teaching that sheds light on veganism is the Four Noble Truths: *dukkha*, the widespread existential state of unsatisfactoriness and suffering; *samudhaya*, the cause and arising of this *dukkha*; *nirodha*, the good news that we can be free of *dukkha*; and *marga*, the Eightfold Path that we can practice in daily life, leading to the extinction of suffering and toward liberation. These two core Buddhist teachings can be seen as comprising essential principles for vegan living as well.

The Five Precepts explicitly includes not just humans, but also animals, in all Buddhist traditions. Animal agriculture is based on exploiting and harming animals – killing them, stealing their sovereignty, time, lives, eggs, milk, and offspring, deceiving them, sexually abusing them, and in most cases, forcing drugs upon them as well. Purchasing, producing, and eating animal-sourced foods and products directly breaks all or most of the five precepts. Veganism is, at its core, an effort to live in compliance with the spirit of nonviolence, *ahimsa*, the foundation of the Five Precepts. Just as Buddhist practice includes nonhuman animals in its sphere of concern, vegan practice endeavors to treat all animals, including humans, with respect and kindness. The Five Precepts teaching clearly mandates vegan living, based on the universal teaching of the Golden Rule. It shines a stark light on our exploitation of animals, illumining discomforting inconsistencies in our culture and personal lives that seem to prompt many of us, including Buddhists, to wear mental sunglasses to reduce the glare.

The Buddha's teaching of the Four Noble Truths can also be applied to vegan living, shedding further light on the connection between Buddhist and vegan practice. The first noble truth of *dukkha* points to the foundational awakening, not just in Buddhism, but also in veganism, which is the necessity of fully realizing the inescapable, (and ultimately unnecessary) suffering at the heart of conditioned existence (for Buddhism), and at the core of our meals and consumerism (for veganism). For Buddhism, this *dukkha* is the underlying, relentless unsatisfactoriness that is unavoidable as long as our minds are operating under the influence of the delusional narrative that we are an objectified, fundamentally separate self. For veganism, the primary concern is with the suffering inflicted on animals by humans. Putting them together, we see that we not only experience suffering due to our delusion, we are further compelled to inflict our suffering and delusion on others, and animals, virtually unprotected, bear the full fury of our projected suffering, delusion, and violence. Delusion, violence, and suffering tend to create more delusion, violence, and suffering, not just for animals and other people, but like a boomerang, for ourselves as well.

The second noble truth of causality is that there is a specific reason for the suffering we experience, and that (for veganism) we inflict on animals. This reason is delusion. We fail to understand our true nature, giving rise to attachment, aversion, manipulativeness, conflict, and unavoidable suffering. Wealth, power, pleasure, prestige, and relationships are ultimately incapable of reducing the unsatisfactoriness of deluded and conditioned awareness, and may even intensify it. Because of our delusion, we fail to see and respect beings as beings, and instead see them as objects to be used, propelling us to mistreat them as means to our ends, sowing seeds of misery for ourselves as well. The third noble truth of cessation is the essential positive truth that we can free ourselves (and animals) from this suffering by awakening from the delusion distorting our perspective. This leads naturally to our yearning to make an effort to awaken, and to the fourth truth, the Eightfold Path. This path applies to the practices of both Buddhism and veganism, and provides concrete teachings and trainings to awaken our mind. *Budh-*, the Sanskrit root, means to awaken. Like Buddhism, veganism is best seen as an ongoing practice of awakening, not as a goal or a state of being, but rather a continual evolution.

The Eightfold Path consists of Right Understanding, Right Aspiration, Right Speech, Right Action, Right Livelihood, Right Effort, Right Mindfulness, and Right Concentration. From the perspective of Buddhism and veganism, right understanding and right aspiration are foundational elements that evolve and develop as we continue our practice. They are paradoxical in this sense. In order to be drawn to and to begin our journey in Buddhism or veganism, we need to have a basically correct view of the situation we, and all beings, are in. We enter our spiritual or vegan path only when our mind and heart ripen sufficiently. This ripening gives rise to an aspiration to awaken ethically and spiritually and to help liberate others. Buddhists teach that even Shakyamuni Buddha is still practicing earnestly, and this reflects the boundless nature of the first two aspects of the Eightfold Path. Right Understanding and Right Aspiration are thus seen not as concrete goals, but as propelling forces that guide and draw practitioners ever onward. They are the fruit, and also the first seed. Buddhist enlightenment is not static, and for veganism, understood as the yearning to treat all beings with kindness and respect, the path is similarly limitless because we can always learn, grow, evolve, and develop in our capacities to be a healing and liberating force for others. This calls us to continually make an effort to refine our understanding and aspiration.

Right speech, action, and livelihood develop out of right understanding and aspiration, and are based on *ahimsa*, non-harmfulness, the foundation for the Five Precepts. As Buddhists—and as vegans—we are called to purify our words, deeds, and livelihoods so that they are in alignment with our understanding and aspiration. For both Buddhists and vegans, this is a calling to speak and act, both inwardly and outwardly, in truthful and respectful ways, refraining from harming or exploiting others, and to have livelihoods that do not lead to our injuring or taking advantage of others, but rather that allow us to benefit them. As in Buddhism, the fundamental principle in vegan living is non-violence. Donald Watson, in coining the word vegan in 1944, broadened and focused the older word vegetarian to include all forms of exploitation and abuse of animals as the foundational motivation, making it essentially equivalent to the ancient word *ahimsa*. Humans are clearly animals also, and so the understanding and aspiration of veganism and Buddhism dovetail in their actual practice, calling us to cultivate kindness and caring in thoughts, words, and deeds in our relations with both humans and animals.

Finally, right effort, mindfulness, and concentration (*samadhi*) are the meditative disciplines and practices that open inner doorways to more fully realize our true nature, freeing us from the imprisoning delusion of being an essentially separate self, and allowing us to liberate ourselves and help liberate others effectively. These last three dimensions of the Eightfold Path call us to a vivid, challenging, and ongoing effort to raise and clarify our awareness, to question the narratives in our mind, and to focus our attention one-pointedly in the reality of the present moment. Each aspect of the Eightfold Path reinforces and develops the others.

While Buddhists have these essential three aspects—right effort, mindfulness, and concentration—built into their foundational teachings, for vegans, these last three have not been recognized as indispensable to the vegan path. However, they should be, and increasing numbers of vegans are realizing that without these inner practices of right effort, mindfulness, and concentration, the ability to embody vegan values of respect, kindness, and freedom is limited by the wounds, programming, and emotional disturbances that condition our awareness and outer actions. It is becoming obvious that effective vegan action, as well as right understanding and aspiration, require inner purification and freedom from deluded self-centeredness, and call us to develop our capacity for intuitive listening and non-distracted attentiveness to the flow of awareness in daily life. The wisdom of the Eightfold Path applies both to the path of vegan liberation of all beings and to the Buddhist path of spiritual awakening. In many ways, the two are different sides of the same coin.

It's interesting that, broadly speaking, two primary traditions, Theravada (the "teaching of the elders") and Mahayana (the "great vehicle"), developed in India and subsequently spread to other parts of Asia, and later to the West. The older Theravada traditions are found today primarily in Thailand, Myanmar, Laos, Cambodia, and Sri Lanka, and are based on the *arhat* ideal. The *arhat*'s aspiration is to attain liberation (*nirvana*) and thus be released from the endless round of suffering in *samsara* (conditioned existence). Mahayana traditions are mainly in China, Vietnam, Korea, Japan, Taiwan, and central Asia, and are based on the *bodhisattva* ideal. The *bodhisattva*'s aspiration is to attain liberation for the benefit of all living beings, and to work tirelessly for the liberation of others from *samsaric* existence. Both Theravada (Vipassana is one familiar form) and Mahayana (Zen is one familiar form) traditions accept and follow the same basic teachings, but it's somewhat intriguing that in the Theravada traditions that emphasize the self-liberation of the *arhat*, meat-eating is quite common, even among monastics. In the Mahayana traditions that stress the *bodhisattva* aspiration of compassion and of working to liberate all living beings, veganism is typically emphasized or required, especially for monastics. The Mahayana tradition developed somewhat later than the original Theravada tradition, and it is primarily the Mahayana sutras, such as the Lankavatara, Surangama, and Mahaparinirvana sutras, that contain the most explicit and unambiguous passages advocating vegan ideals, though these sutras are, for the most part, disregarded by Theravadans.

As some of the essays in this volume elucidate, Buddhism has been a worldwide force encouraging compassion toward both animals and humans, and encouraging vegan living. When, for example, emperor Asoka converted to Buddhism in third century BCE India, he renounced his warlike ways and helped usher in an era of greater cultural harmony and peace that extended to animals by promoting vegetarianism and an extensive network of animal-care facilities. The Buddhist teachings have always unequivocally supported vegan living, which is now increasingly understood to be the essential foundation for a more conscious world where justice, harmony, health, sustainability, and abundance are possible.

We are seeing in recent decades a resurgence of vegan teachings within many Buddhist lineages and traditions. This seems to be driven by grassroots pressure from the laity and younger monastics to honor the ethical and spiritual root teachings and to question the tendency to westernize Buddhist practice. For me, personally, traveling through China, Taiwan, Korea, and Vietnam, lecturing on vegan living and working with Buddhist monasteries and centers, it was refreshing to be working with religious institutions striving actively and creatively to promote veganism and respect for animals in the general culture. We rarely see this in the West, where the three Abrahamic religions that were formed under the knife of animal agriculture typically fail to question, and instead often promote, the relentless killing and abuse of animals that define our world today. We are also seeing an increased interest in, and commitment to, veganism in Theravada and Tibetan traditions. Orgyen Trinley Dorje, the young 17th Karmapa and head of the Kagyu lineage, for example, strongly discourages lamas in the lineage from eating meat.

It's essential to note that the vegetarianism that is practiced and promoted by Buddhist teachers, while being a step in the right direction, still fails to fully honor the precepts against killing and harming others. Leather, wool, silk, and other products require abusing and killing animals. Milk and egg products also invariably entail killing, sexual abuse, and stealing animals' offspring and secretions, as well as their sovereignty and purposes. This is true of so-called organic, free-range, and humane operations as well, as numerous studies and investigations have demonstrated. Even putting aside the abuse, theft, and usual killing involved, owning other living beings as property is inherently harmful to them and contradictory to the Dharma.

Animal agriculture, the living core of the culture into which we have all been born, is the epitome of samsaric delusion manifesting as violence, disease, exploitation, and war. We have all been wounded by our upbringing, whatever our current religious and consumption orientation may be. How can we bring healing to ourselves and our situation here? How can we best question herderism's narratives and practices within us, and in our culture, and co-create a world more in alignment with our values and inner wisdom? What role can Buddhist and vegan teachings and practice play in our personal and cultural evolution?

This present volume attempts to illuminate these questions by exploring both the theory and the practice of Buddhism and veganism as they influence each other and blend to help create positive change in our world. Many of the essays provide personal stories illustrating how Buddhist and vegan practice reinforce and deepen each other.

Thank you for your interest in these questions and for your efforts to address the urgent situation we are all facing today. The ancient teaching of *ahimsa*—at the core of both Buddhist and vegan practice—lives in all of us as inherent compassion and wisdom. May we unfold these capacities within us for the benefit of all living beings.

# Vegan Dharma

DAVID BLATTE

My introduction to the Dharma came at the tender age of twelve – although I didn't recognize it as such at the time. My parents and I were on a road trip during winter vacation – they were both teachers – and one day my father drove by himself to visit a student of his who lived nearby. He had still not returned when I went to sleep, and a few hours later I was awakened by a loud knock on the hotel room door. A policeman stood there, giving us the news that my father had been killed in a car accident.

I was, in an instant, completely immersed in *dukkha* (suffering), aware not only of my own sadness and confusion but also the relentless agony of my mother, whose uncontrollable sobs resonated through the house for what seemed like months. Over time, as my own pain diminished and I again looked outward, I started to view the world around me in a new light. Suffering was not confined to me, my mother, or those affected by my father's death. Nor was it unique to humans. As I observed the animals and insects on our wooded property, I understood that they too did not escape suffering. I could not know the exact nature of their experience, but that they suffered was inescapable. They avoided harm just as desperately as humans, and even the tiniest insects seemed to fear for their lives – a centipede rolling up into a ball or a mosquito avoiding a swat. In this, my family, my species, and I myself were not alone. There was a bond shared by all sentient beings, large and small, forged in our common experience of suffering.

It was not long after this realization that I stopped intentionally killing insects. Then, in college, when anti-fur protests were at their zenith, another student equated wearing fur – which I passionately opposed – with eating meat, pointing out that while one was for vanity and the other for sensual pleasure, neither was necessary, and both were dependent on the killing of an animal. The logic was compelling, so I became a vegetarian. Ten years later, while in law school, when I was exposed to factory farms and saw the suffering inherent in eating eggs and dairy, I became vegan. I was also fortunate to have Gary Francione, an animal law attorney and professor, take me on as an intern. In 2000, I served as executive director of Vegan Action, known for its institution of a popular vegan logo, and after that I started my own animal law practice, which I maintained for five years. My concern for the well-being of animals has permeated my personal and professional life for over 45 years.

I was first formally introduced to the Dharma in college where, as a philosophy major, I studied Eastern religions. Recently, I discovered a paper I had written and I could see that the instruction had been substantial. In it I discussed the three characteristics – impermanence, suffering, and not-self – and analyzed the distinction between Theravada and Mahayana Buddhism. About ten years later, I had a brief foray into Transcendental Meditation. Finally, around the age of forty, when I moved to Berkeley, California, I explored a number of traditions and settled on my current practice, which I've maintained for twenty years.

My present path began with a beginner's course by James Baraz, a teacher affiliated with Spirit Rock Meditation Center, a Theravada center whose method is based on the *Satipatthana Sutta*, which discusses the four foundations of mindfulness. One experience in particular still stands out in my mind – being introduced to the First Precept: Do not kill. Importantly, do not kill *animals*. I remember my elation the moment I came across this teaching that included all sentient beings, not just humans, in its field of concern. I had finally found a philosophy that shared my deep and long-held conviction that all sentient life, regardless of species, is to be respected.

Over the next two years, as my practice developed, I naturally assumed that my teachers and fellow students were vegetarian, just as the food at events and retreats was vegetarian. It never occurred to me that they were not. My rude awakening came at the end of a ten-day retreat with one of my favorite teachers when, going to say goodbye, I found him eating his lunch – a fish. I was shocked. Since then I've come to learn that most lay practitioners and teachers, and perhaps even most monks, are not vegetarians, let alone vegans. But at the time it was quite jarring. What I took for granted as an indispensable element of the practice was apparently more the exception than the norm.

My dual pursuits as an advocate for animals and as a meditator came together in 2004 when, at the end of a three-month retreat at Insight Mediation Society, I found myself talking to another retreatant, Bob Isaacson, and quickly found we had much in common. In addition to being former public interest defense attorneys (he was a death penalty lawyer and I a public defender) and sharing a commitment to the Dharma and to animals, we were both disappointed and perplexed that so many of our fellow practitioners ate animals. We continued the conversation when we returned home, and before long, along with Patti Breitman and Kim Sturla, formed Dharma Voices for Animals, an organization dedicated to raising awareness of animal suffering and abuse, with an emphasis on a plant-based diet, within the meditation/Buddhist community. The organization continues to grow, hopefully preparing the way for the time when all practitioners fully embrace the ethic of non-harm.

After the IMS retreat, as my commitment to the practice continued to grow deeper, I decided to leave my home, law practice, and partner, and bought a one-way ticket to Pa Auk Monastery in Myanmar. The teacher, Pa Auk Sayadaw, emphasized the development of concentration – specifically the *jhanas* – something in which I had always felt I was not sufficiently strong. But what really drew me to Pa Auk was that Sayadaw, and the monastery itself, was vegetarian. As I subsequently learned, Sayadaw places a great emphasis on morality (*sila*), setting an example by the life he leads.

The time in Myanmar, and subsequently at Na Uyana Monastery in Sri Lanka, was transformative. I was exposed to an entirely different relationship to the Dharma. For monks, meditation has a singular purpose – the attainment of *nibbana* (nirvana, enlightenment), which is the only and ultimate freedom from suffering. I quickly embraced that goal, and while not an ordained monk, the Dharma remains my guiding principle and the attainment of *nibbana* my primary pursuit.

Few people, at least in my culture, are raised vegetarian or vegan, and each person's path leading to the decision to refrain from eating animals is unique and forged by a combination of emotional and intellectual influences often at odds with each other. From a Buddhist perspective, the inquiry begins with a comprehensive examination of the scriptures, both as they address animals directly and as they illuminate universal truths that guide our behavior. When it comes to the foundational teachings, the two major lineages – Mahayana and Theravada – are identical. There is no disagreement that the First Precept's edict of not-killing extends to animals as well as humans. As the Buddha says in the Theravadan *Cula-hatthipadopama Sutta*:

> When he has thus gone forth, endowed with the monks' training and livelihood, then — abandoning the taking of life — he abstains from the taking of life. He dwells with his rod laid down, his knife laid down, scrupulous, merciful, compassionate for the welfare of all living beings.

Not only should one not kill, but one should not cause another to be killed. In the *Dhammapada*, verse 129, the Buddha instructed:

> All tremble at the rod; all are fearful of death.
> Drawing the parallel to yourself, neither kill nor
> get others to kill.

The qualities of compassion and loving-kindness are extolled in both lineage's scriptures, with the traditional Theravada *metta* (loving-kindness) meditation serving as a mainstay of many modern practices. Right livelihood in both traditions prohibits trade in living beings and in animal flesh. Other shared teachings, such as that all beings have at one time been your mother, and the workings of karma in which killing animals leads to a rebirth either as a creeping animal or in the hell realms, also lead to the conclusion that eating animals is inconsistent with the Dharma.

It is in the specific teachings about eating animals where the two lineages diverge. In the Mahayana scriptures, the prohibition against eating animals is unequivocal, stated explicitly and repeatedly. For example, in the *Lankavatara Sutra* the Buddha instructs:

> Thus, Mahamati, whenever and wherever there is evolution among sentient beings, let people cherish the thought of kinship with them, and holding the thought intention of treating them as if they were our only child, and therefore refrain from eating their flesh.
>
> So much more should Bodhisattvas, who are committed to being compassionate towards all sentient beings, and whose inner nature is compassion itself, choose to refrain from eating animal flesh.

The subject is also addressed in the *Mahaparinirvana Sutra*:

> There is no animal flesh to be regarded as pure by any exception. It does not matter if the giving of animal flesh for us to eat is premeditated or not, asked for or not, or whether extreme hunger is present or not. Therefore it is wise to not eat animal flesh in any circumstance which naturally arises within our life.
>
> Let yogis not eat any animal flesh.
>
> Animal flesh eating is forbidden by me everywhere and for all time for those who abide in compassion.

Some Mahayana teachings go further, suggesting veganism as the wise practice, as discussed in the *Surangama Sutra*:

How can a *bhikkshu*, who hopes to become a deliverer of others, himself be living on the flesh of other sentient beings? Pure and earnest *bhikkshus*, if they are earnest and sincere, will never wear clothing made of silk, nor wear boots made of leather, because it involves the taking of life.

The Theravada scriptures, however, provide no such clarity, and there are some instances, according to the *vinaya* (monastic code) and discourses, where the Buddha accepts and eats animals. The main teaching on the eating of animals is a principle known as the three purities found, among other places, in the *Jivaka Sutta*, where the Buddha responds to the accusation that he eats animals killed for him:

Jivaka, I say that there are three instances in which meat should not be eaten: when it is seen, heard, or suspected [that the living being has been slaughtered for the *bhikkhu*]. I say that meat should not be eaten in these three instances. I say that there are three instances in which meat may be eaten: when it is not seen, not heard, and not suspected [that the living being has been slaughtered for the *bhikkhu*]. I say that meat may be eaten in these three instances.

Much could be questioned about this doctrine, including its authenticity, but even if taken as authentic, its purpose was not to generally condone the eating of animals but instead to narrowly proscribe circumstances under which this was allowed – when the eating of an animal does not contribute to the killing of an animal. It's also significant that this instruction was aimed specifically at monks who then, as now, relied on alms for their food. Most modern laypeople have any number of choices when going to a market or restaurant.

There's a common misconception articulated when meat -eaters, both monastics and laypeople, sometimes say that they are simply taking what is offered. The Buddha never gave the instruction to eat what is offered without inquiry or consideration of the moral implications. On the contrary. In a story in the *vinaya*, a woman named Suppiya cuts off a piece of her thigh to make broth for a sick monk, who unknowingly eats it. The Buddha reprimands the monk, saying "Nor, monks, should you make use of flesh without inquiring about it." Just as a monk would not consume alcohol simply because it is offered, he should not simply accept meat. Eating, like all of our actions, has moral implications, and the question for the three purities is whether by eating an animal you are causing an animal to be killed, and the answer in virtually every instance is yes.

While the teachings are certainly instructive, in my experience the decision to eat or refrain from eating animals is a much more complicated process than a simple scriptural analysis. Food plays a pre-eminent role in our lives, satisfying not only our physical needs, but also impacting our emotional and psychological ones. Whether through karma, DNA, or societal influences, most of us are deeply conditioned to eat animals. In many ways the spiritual practice of Buddhism is a process of re-conditioning, and we all know how difficult that is. When we are faced with the question of whether or not to continue to eat animals, there are ingrained and often unrecognized patterns that inform our decision and potentially act as hindrances to eating wisely. We need look no further than the Dalai Lama, an occasional meat-eater who admits to an inability to abide by his own lineage's teachings. It is one thing to know the right thing, and quite another to do it.

In the end, it may all come down to one simple fact – people like eating meat. We desire, even crave it, and like most desires we don't want to give it up. The very thought of renouncing meat can produce an onslaught of unpleasant emotions, including a profound sense of loss. I remember how difficult it was when I made the transition to a vegetarian diet. But over time, not just with meat but as with many forms of renunciation, a transformation occurs. Rather than being borne as a burden, it is experienced as liberating. One feels the bliss of freedom both from desire and from any vestige of moral blameworthiness. For many, what was formerly a desire to eat meat is replaced by an aversion to do so. While this may have the effect of replacing one unwholesome root with another, at least the only suffering you cause is your own.

The Buddha obviously understood the power of desire, and he anticipated that people would be resistant to the practice of not eating animals. He discussed this in the *Mahayana Mahaparinirvana Sutra*:

> Let a person not give power to the many rationalizations given to justify animal flesh eating. What logicians say under the influence of their addictive craving for animal flesh is sophistic, delusional, and argumentative. What they imagine that they witnessed, heard, or suspected that the Blessed One has said, or another Buddha said or did, is grossly distorted.
>
> As greed is a hindrance to liberation, so are the objects of greed a hindrance to liberation. Objects of greed like animal flesh eating and consuming alcohol are hindrances to liberation.
>
> A time may come when deluded people may say, "Animal flesh is appropriate food to eat, has no karmic consequences, and is permitted by the Buddha."
>
> Some will even say that eating animal flesh can be medicinal. It is more like eating the flesh of your only child. Let a yogi be attuned to what

is balanced and nourishing to eat, be adverse to consuming animal flesh and alcohol, and with this clarity go about peacefully begging for food, trusting that what is wanted and needed to sustain a healthy life will be supplied.

As with all of the teachings, each person must determine for herself or himself the right path when it comes to eating animals. It is a question that demands an open and honest inquiry and an unflinching willingness to face dukkha head-on, both our own and that of others. It requires that we confront our limitations and, if we are to live the practice, put our beliefs into action, however uncomfortable that may be. My hope is that in making this inquiry, others reach the conclusion I've reached – that eating animals and animal products is inconsistent with the Dharma, and that wisdom, in today's world, means adopting a plant-based diet and lifestyle.

# Buddhism and Vegetarianism: What the Sutras State

TONY PAGE

Buddhism and vegetarianism constitute for me one great, integrated path, the path of compassion, kindliness and peace. I owe my Buddhism to vegetarianism and my vegetarianism to Buddhism. How did that come about?

Ever since my childhood in Kennington, London, I have always felt an instinctive love for, and rapport with, animals. I remember an old hen who used to wander around a neighbour's garden and who would not allow anyone to touch her; she would bite their fingers if they tried. I, a little six-year-old boy, was the only person in the neighbourhood that this old hen would permit to stroke and caress her.

I regarded animals as my friends. I viewed them as "people," just as any human being whom I had ever encountered and I took a delight in trying to make them happy. A cat's purring would fill me with joy. To know that I held in my hands the power of bringing happiness to other sentient beings was an awe-inspiring and soul-enriching thought for me.

Like many children, I had an instinctive aversion to meat. My parents had to force me to eat the hateful stuff. Sadly, this enforced and ingrained habit lasted until I was a student at Oxford University in the early 1980s. It was then that, with a growing awareness of animal rights awakening within me, I came upon a small, life-changing book entitled *A Buddhist Case for Vegetarianism* by the American Zen monk, Roshi Philip Kapleau. His vivid and harrowing descriptions of the terror that animals experience as they are dragged into the slaughter-house, smelling the blood and death that awaits them, so horrified and appalled me that I decided there and then that I no longer wished to be a part of this monstrous and murderous system. I became a Buddhist and a vegetarian the very next day. Much later, I would become a vegan.

That book by Roshi Philip Kapleau radically changed my life. It led me deeply both into vegetarianism and Buddhism to which I had already been introduced to some extent by the late celebrated English Buddhist, Justice Christmas Humphreys. I would never look back. In fact, in 1999 (if I might be permitted a moment's lapse into immodesty!) I wrote what turned out to be the first large-scale study of Buddhism and animal rights, *Buddhism and Animals: A Buddhist Vision of Humanity's Rightful Relationship with the Animal Kingdom.*

Now, a couple of decades later, I can reflect upon a journey of exploration into the Buddhist suttas and sutras which give a solid spiritual underpinning to my instinctive vegetarianism and to veganism as well.

Where to begin? Shortage of space compels me to mention only a few scriptural examples of the Buddha's disapprobation of meat consumption; there is much more that could be cited. Let me start with the *Pali* suttas, the basis of Theravada Buddhism. These are the reputedly earliest record of the Buddha's teachings that we have. What do they say?

Most Theravadins believe that meat eating is permitted by the suttas, while others say carnivorism is a transgression of the spirit of the Dharma, the spiritual Truth. The second view would seem to be the more logical of the two.

In the *Jivakasutta* of the *Majjhima-Nikaya*, the Buddha states: "I ... say that in three cases, meat may not be used: if it is seen, heard, suspected."[1] Meat-eating Buddhists usually gloss over this passage. They say that it is acceptable for a Buddhist monk to eat meat if he has not seen, heard or suspected that the animal was killed especially for himself. However, a much more natural and unforced reading would be that a monk should not eat meat if he sees, hears or suspects that an item of food presented to him is actually meat (some non-flesh foods, after all, such as certain mushrooms, can strongly resemble meat in appearance, and meat and fish can hide in sauces and stews.)

Of course, the ethical basis of refraining from meat consumption draws its power from the first Buddhist precept, which is to 'refrain from the taking of life.' By paying others to slay animals and supply their flesh to us, we are, from a moral standpoint, complicit in the taking of animal life. It should thus be obvious from this perspective alone that Buddhism cannot logically endorse the eating of meat.

When we come to Mahayana Buddhism, the Buddha's disapprobation of meat consumption is much clearer. In the *Mahayana Mahaparinirvana Sutra,* the bodhisattva Kasyapa comments to the Buddha: "In my view, there is great virtue in not eating meat."[2] The Buddha replies:

> Excellent, excellent! You have now reached a clear understanding of my point. The bodhisattva who protects the dharma [spiritual Truth] should be like this ... from today I establish a precept restricting my disciples from eating all forms of meat.[3]

Kasyapa specifically asks the Buddha why he does not allow the eating of meat. The Buddha explains with the following succinct asseveration: "to eat meat is to cut out the seeds of your own great compassion."[4] As is well known, compassion is one of the highest virtues and *desiderata* in all Buddhism so to extirpate the seeds of such compassion is tantamount to committing spiritual suicide.

In this same sutra, the Buddha also reveals that destructively minded, truth-averse persons have reversed the Buddha's teaching on meat consumption and substituted a lie instead:

> People such as these will destroy the rules of discipline, the proper practices, and the dignity and decorum that have been formulated by the Tathagata [i.e. the Buddha]. They will preach the goal of liberation and avoiding impurities, even as they destroy the teaching that is profound and hidden. Having reached the point where each of them follows his or her own ideas, they will make assertions in opposition to what is in the sutras and *vinayas* [rules for monks] such as, 'Tathagatas [i.e. Buddhas] all allow us to eat meat.'[5]

In the *Mahaparinirvana Sutra*, further, the Buddha even makes reference to the sensitivity of animals when he speaks of their pulling away in horror and fright from humans who eat animal flesh. The animals can smell the odour of death that emanates from meat eaters:

> ... those [humans] who do partake of meat, whether they are walking, standing, sitting, or lying down, will produce an odor of meat that all living beings will smell and this inevitably creates a sense of fear in them ...Any living being who smells the scent of meat will become afraid and will be filled with the fear of death. All forms of life, whether they live out their lives in water, on land, or in the air, flee from [this smell]. They will all say: 'This person is our enemy.' For this reason, bodhisattvas do not customarily eat meat.[6]

Perhaps the most uncompromising and powerful denunciation by the Buddha of meat eating is to be found in the *Lankavatara Sutra*. Here the Buddha gives the lie to the claim that it is acceptable to eat meat if one has not killed the animal oneself or had another kill it for one. The Buddha rejects this specious line of reasoning in one fell swoop, saying: "If ... meat is not eaten by anybody for any reason, there will be no destroyer of life."[7] Right! It is because of the demand from the flesh-imbibing public for meat, that meat continues to be supplied, and as a consequence animals continue to be murdered. It is as simple as that.

The *Lankavatara Sutra* gives a number of reasons as to why one should not eat flesh, including the core ground of compassion for all living creatures. The Buddha ends his excursus with unequivocal words to Bodhisattva, Mahamati:

> ... in the present sutra all [meat] in any form, in any manner, and in any place, is unconditionally and once for all, prohibited for all. Thus, Mahama-

ti, meat-eating I have not permitted to anyone, I do
not permit, I will not permit.[8]

Strong words. There can be no mistaking the Buddha's moral outrage at the very notion of slaying and feasting on the bodies of sensitive, sentient beings. But why, more precisely, should we respect such sentient beings and refrain from killing them?

The *Angulimaliya Sutra* (a *Mahayana* sutra that is not to be confused with the similarly titled one from the *Pali suttas*) gives us the answer. It links such abstention to the profound teaching of the *Buddha-dhātu* or *Tathāgata-garbha*, the Buddha Nature or Buddha Essence, the living spiritual organ or element immanent within all beings. He tells Mañjuśrī, the great Bodhisattva of Wisdom, that to take the lives of others is to destroy one's own spiritual core, and that a Buddha is one who refrains from such a practice:

> He who has abandoned the taking of life because it
> is the *dhātu* of all beings is a Buddha. Noble son,
> taking life in the world is like killing oneself, for it
> destroys one's *dhātu*.[9]

Mañjuśrī then asks, "Do Buddhas not eat meat because of the *tathāgata-garbha*?" The Buddha replies, explaining that we are all interrelated members of one family stretching back through seemingly endless and beginningless time in the cycles of reincarnation, and that we are each of us composed of one spiritual element, the 'Buddha *Dhātu* (Buddha Essence), shared with all other beings:

> Mañjuśrī, that is so. There are no beings who have
> not been one's mother, who have not been one's
> sister through generations of wandering in begin-
> ningless and endless *samsāra*. Even one who is a

dog has been one's father, for the world of living
beings is like a dancer. Therefore, one's own flesh
and the flesh of another are a single flesh, so Buddhas do not eat meat.

Moreover, Mañjuśrī, the *dhātu* of all beings
is the *dharmadhātu* [spiritual Totality], so Buddhas
do not eat meat because they would be eating the
flesh of one single *dhātu*."[10]

This is a fascinating revelation. By eating meat we are actually descending into cannibalism! So, what about veganism?
Is there any support for it in the Buddhist sutras? Yes, there is.
The Buddha tended to teach in gradations of spiritual and moral
intensity, tailoring his messages according to the levels of attainment of his auditors, from the basic to the more complex and
ethically lofty. Thus, while vegetarianism is taught in many of
the *Mahayana sutras*, it would appear that veganism is the ideal
to move toward as promulgated in the *Surangama Sutra*, one of
the spiritually richest of all *Mahayana sutras*, where the Buddha
asks and answers his own question:

How ... can you eat the flesh of living beings and
so pretend to be my disciple? ...

All bhiksus [Buddhist monks] who live
purely and all Bodhisattvas always refrain even from
walking on the grass; how can they agree to uproot
it? How then can those who practise great compassion feed on the flesh and blood of living beings? If
bhiksus do not wear garments made of silk, boots of
local leather and furs, and refrain from consuming
milk, cream and butter, they will really be liberated
from the worldly; after paying their former debts,
they will not transmigrate in the three realms of
existence. Why? Because by using animal products,

one creates causes, just like a man who eats cereals grown in the soil and whose feet cannot leave the ground. If a man can (control) his body and mind and thereby refrains from eating animal flesh and wearing animal products, I say he will really be liberated. This teaching of mine is that of the Buddha whereas any other is that of evil demons.[11]

Thus to liberate animals from exploitation and murder is to spiritually liberate ourselves.

It has been my own experience, and that of many others, that the active expansion of one's heartfelt compassion towards animals first begins with vegetarianism, and then veganism, and then as a consequence embraces opposition to such practices as vivisection, experimentation on living animals. Vivisection is often defended by its promoters as a practice that is compassionate towards human beings, as it allegedly provides cures for human ailments and relieves humans of their suffering under all forms of sickness. This is a propagandistic lie of the most heinous kind.

First, the physiological and anatomical differences and unexpected, unpredictable enzymatic and general biological variations between animals and humans are so great that one can never reliably extrapolate findings from any given animal test to a human being. It is like experimenting on cheetahs and hoping to gain valid results applicable to sloths! One simply cannot reliably extrapolate physiological data across the species barrier. Just one example from my book, *Vivisection Unveiled*: in the course of my research into the subject of live-animal experimentation, I established (from my study of vivisectors' own experimentation records) that rabbits can survive a dose of deadly strychnine *30 times greater* (relative to body weight) than would kill a human being![12] With variations of biological response on this scale, and there are others which are even more astounding, who can place any reliance on animals tests for the safety and efficacy of our medicines and chemicals?

Second, even if vivisection *were* a scientifically and methodologically sound practice for the acquiring of human knowledge in the fields of human health and therapeutics (which it emphatically is not), would that give us the right to brutalise, torture and kill those creatures who have done us no harm and who are powerless to fight back? Clearly not. Trying to help one sentient being by slaughtering another is no way to move forward on a spiritual path, or even on a decent human path. It is a contradiction of all moral and spiritual logic.

I would like to close with the assurance that if you are a practising Buddhist, or are interested in this expression of altruistic spirituality, then vegetarianism and on to veganism is the route to go. By trying one's best to refrain from the terrorising and slaughter of innocent lives, one is drawing closer to the divine Buddha that indwells the heart of each and every sentient being.

Thank you to the indefatigable Dr. Will Tuttle for giving me the opportunity to share with you these thoughts and such little knowledge as I possess.

**References:**
1. *Jivakasutta* of the *Majjhima-Nikaya*, tr. by I. B. Horner as *The Middle Length Sayings*, Pali Text Society, London, 1957, p. 33.
2. *The Nirvana Sutra*, Volume 1, tr. by Mark L. Blum, Bukkyo Dendo Kyokai America, 2013, p. 110.
3. *The Nirvana Sutra*, op. cit., pp. 110 – 112.
4. *The Nirvana Sutra*, op. cit., p. 111.
5. *The Nirvana Sutra*, op. cit., p. 113.
6. *The Nirvana Sutra*, op. cit., pp. 112-113.
7. *The Lankavatara Sutra* tr. by Dr. D. T. Suzuki, Prajna Press, Boulder, 1978, p. 217.
8. *The Lankavatara Sutra*, op. cit., p. 219.
9. *The Angulimaliya Sutra*, tr. by Buddhist scholar Stephen Hodge for the present author, as yet unpublished.
10. *The Angulimaliya Sutra*, tr. by Stephen Hodge.
11. *The Surangama Sutra*, tr. by Lu K'uan Yü, B. I. Publications, Bombay, 1978, pp. 153 – 154.
12. *Vivisection Unveiled*, Jon Carpenter Publications, Oxford, 1997, p. 10.

# Vegetarianism in Chinese Buddhism

PROFESSOR GONG JUN

The year 517 saw a landmark in the history of Chinese Buddhism when a congress of Buddhist monks was convened by the famous Buddhist emperor of the Liang Dynasty, Xiao Yan. The purpose of this meeting was to bring together all the eminent Buddhist monks to discuss the issue of endorsing the precept of prohibiting wine and meat consumption within the Buddhist order. As a result, a ban on wine and meat was promulgated in the form of a state administrative decree. From then on, vegetarianism has gradually developed into the basic custom for Chinese Buddhism, which applies to all the monks and nuns in terms of spiritual practice and daily life. This Chinese Buddhist vegetarianism typically includes abstaining from dairy products and eggs, which are seen as part of meat farming, as well as from leather, silk, fur, and other products derived from animals.

The controversy that occurred in the sixth century over the relation of non-killing and vegetarianism to the doctrines of Buddhism is of historical significance, because the resulting congress had a profound and enduring impact on the development of Chinese Buddhism in later times. Not only has it determined the essential role of vegetarianism which characterizes Chinese Buddhism, but has also shaped a variety of customs and rituals in the secular life of the Chinese people of today.

Buddhism originated in India. As far as the doctrine of primitive Indian Buddhism is concerned, we do not find a strict prohibition of meat-eating in the precepts of the early Theravada Buddhism. The ban on meat, as seen in Chinese Buddhism, is related mainly to the thought of Mahayana Buddhism as it developed in India. The introduction of Buddhism to China centered on the teachings of Mahayana Buddhism in which vegetarianism is clearly indicated, as seen in the famous Mahayana sutras such as *Lankavatara Sutra*, *Nirvana Sutra*, *Mahavaipulya-Buddhavatamska Sutra*, *Surangam Sutra*, *Angulimaliya Sutra*, and others.

All of the aforementioned sacred texts expressly proclaim the concept of vegetarianism on the basis of compassion. These teachings indicate that the Buddhist idea of compassion as well as the ideal of monastic life are closely linked with the prohibition of meat. For example, in the *Lankavatara Sutra* the necessity of prohibiting meat is particularly addressed in one passage that reads, "flesh and blood are abandoned by the immortals and being excluded from the diet of the holy men, therefore Bodhisattvas should never eat meat," and "meat-eating causes all kinds of obstacles which prevent one from any spiritual accomplishment, therefore Bodhisattvas who intend to help themselves and others should never eat meat." The *Nirvana Sutra* says,

> Do not eat meat, do not drink wine, adjust the mind so as to reap the fruit of Dharma. Take seriously the retribution of your deeds, be they good or evil; whatever has been done, the consequences will follow just like the shadow follows the object. The cycle of cause and retribution runs ceaselessly in the past, present and future. Should you pass this life in futility, nothing can be done to get it back and you will deeply regret it.

Here it is clearly pointed out that meat as unclean or impure food not only does harm to our body and mind, but will also directly impede our spiritual accomplishment as Buddhist practitioners. These renowned Mahayana sutras have played a pivotal role in the Chinese Buddhist world. Thus the notion that a Buddhist practitioner should keep a meat-free diet became essential to Chinese Buddhism from the early days of Buddhism's arrival in China.

Chinese Buddhists do not regulate their religious life in accordance with the early sutras of precepts as shown in Theravada Buddhism. The prevailing code of ethics is dominated by the *Brahmajala Sutra*, in which the provisions of vegetarianism are clearly put forward: "Do not eat any meat. A carnivore has ruined his great compassionate seeds of Buddha nature, and all sentient beings will avoid seeing him. Thus Bodhisattvas should not eat the flesh of any sentient beings, and eating meat incurs countless sins." A sutra of precepts like this one tells us that vegetarianism is the basic requirement of the Buddhist ideal of a compassionate life. Should one contradict the principle of compassion, one cannot become a qualified Buddhist. It is not difficult to understand why the ideas and normative codes prevalent in Chinese Buddhist circles have a clear ban on meat, which is rare in other Buddhist traditions around the world.

Researchers have found that the formation of the vegetarian tradition in Chinese Buddhism was not merely due to its reception of the requirements of Mahayana Buddhism, but more importantly to its integration with the indigenous traditions of Confucianism and Taoism in China. Even before Buddhism was introduced into China, the idea of benevolence and altruism had been foreshadowed by the teachings of Confucianism and Taoism. For example, in Confucianism it is said that "a gentleman keeps away from his slaughter-house and cook-room," and "having heard their [the animals'] dying cries, he cannot bear to eat their flesh." Taoist advocacy of naturalism also expressed the notion of respect, love and forgiveness for all lives, including animals. Thus non-killing sacrifices and offerings became a custom in Chinese folk life. It is also part of Chinese tradition that "one should fast in order to serve the ghosts and spirits" in the seasons of sacrifice, and on significant days such as solar and lunar eclipses. Additionally, China's earliest medical book, *The Inner Canon of Emperors* puts forward a theory of health care that advocates "grains for nourishment, and fruits for supplement." These factors may help explain why the precept of requiring a meat-free diet is not universally present in other Buddhist traditions around the world, and it is only in the field of Chinese Buddhism that the prohibition of meat-eating has become so important an issue and is whole-heartedly accepted.

That Chinese Buddhists boldly and clearly call for vegetarianism is also related to their understanding and interpretation of Buddhist doctrines. Chinese Buddhists take compassion as the fundamental ethical teaching of Buddhism, which should be extended to all "sentient beings" including animals. Thus, killing animals for their flesh is the most serious and fundamental subversion of this principle. Unlike other Buddhist traditions, among the precepts of Chinese Buddhism, the prohibition of killing is placed above all the other precepts, hence the ban on meat acquires a deep religious significance. A carnivorous diet, according to the tradition of Chinese Buddhism, absolutely blocks one's way to spiritual achievement.

In addition, the act of eating meat is treated as a violation of the Buddhist law of causality. This can be illustrated by the example of the aforementioned Buddhist emperor. One important reason for his proposition of forsaking meat is that he believed that meat-eating itself is the cause for ignorance, retribution and calamities, and in his own words "eating the flesh of sentient beings is the cause of all sorts of suffering and disease."

For Chinese Buddhists, one must first become a vegetarian to be liberated from the suffering of human life. Vegetarianism remains essential to Chinese Buddhism to this day. In the Ming Dynasty it is readdressed by the eminent Buddhist monk, the Lotus-Pool master Zhu Hong in the form of poetry. His famous poem, "Seven Stroke Liquidation," thoroughly expounded his view that meat-eating will cause endless grievances and unfortunate reincarnations, hence non-vegetarian dishes should be abandoned. Further, these endless grievances are also the root of all wars. Chinese Buddhists believe that "in the food we eat lies our grievance and hatred; if you want to know the reason for war, just go to the butcher's house and listen to the cries at midnight." This is a famous saying throughout China. Vegetarianism therefore is a peaceful diet or diet for peace in the sense that it offers the only lasting solution to war for the nation and the people.

There is a popular saying in China that the mouth is the entrance of disease, meaning that diet is the first major destroyer of health. This notion is likely to be one that has evolved from Buddhism. In Chinese Buddhism, the ban on meat can be explained in both spiritual and medical terms. From the aspect of physical nutrition, the notion of "uncleanness or impurity" is proposed. It affirms that meat is not clean and does harm to our health. Thus we have the saying that "blood and flesh pave the way for one hundred diseases," while vegetables make us "full of energy" and benefit us in many ways (Buddhist emperor Xiao Yan, "Ban on Wine and Meat").

This concept conforms to what is stated in the Mahayana sutras such as the *Lankavatara Sutra* that says the body of a meat-eater "usually contains lots of wild worms, and is likely to have sore psoriasis, tuberculoid leprosy, and many other diseases which are symptoms of uncleanness." In summary, vegetarianism has been thoroughly discussed in Chinese Buddhism and has been fully expounded from the aspects of physical and mental health. The notion of vegetarianism in Chinese Buddhism also emphasizes the importance of keeping a "vegetarian mind," meaning that the sense of compassion and *ahimsa* is the fundamental principle of vegetarianism.

As stated in the early Buddhist sutras, Buddha allowed his disciples to eat meat in certain special circumstances, which is the so-called "three net meat" (not personally seeing the animals being slaughtered or hearing their cries at the moment of being killed, and that animals are not killed for the eater's sake.) This concept has influenced Theravada Buddhism and the traditions of Mongolian and Tibetan Buddhism. They believe the precept of vegetarianism was not particularly stressed by Buddha himself, and the life of a mendicant cannot afford it, because whatever the donor offered should be received with appreciation. Hence Buddhism is not seen as a tradition that particularly advocates vegetarianism.

Pedagogically speaking, the Buddha indeed highlighted the positive side with regard to his teaching of compassion and ahimsa. He inclined to teach his disciples by his own example, and to furnish followers the opportunity to get the point on their own. Because Buddhism attaches significance to practice, when the meaning of compassion is genuinely understood by a practitioner, his body and mind will automatically refuse any kind of harmful food. Besides, it is not the Buddha's manner to use a coercive way to regulate others, and he preferred to provide his disciples with some positive guidance. For that reason, the teaching of compassion and ahimsa is highlighted, whereas the precept is "gradually endorsed according to the demand of situations." This means that when something harmful is committed to the extent that it has affected the whole sangha and may have an impact on the reputation of the monks, the Buddha would take some action to prevent it reoccurring, and thus precepts have been gradually formally introduced only as necessary.

This style of Buddha's pedagogy has been well received by the Chinese Buddhists who wisely interpreted this controversial matter with their own words. An interesting question related to Chinese Buddhist vegetarianism is that Chinese Buddhists have developed a unique and ingenious understanding and interpretation of such a change regarding Buddha's teaching of vegetarianism. Basically, it has changed from tolerating meat in the early days of Indian Buddhism to strictly prohibiting meat and fervently advocating vegetarianism in Mahayana Buddhism. They argue that Buddha introduced the precepts into the sangha step-by-step, meaning in the early days Buddha's focus was on the so-called "convenient way" in spreading the Dharma, hence allowing the disciples to eat meat in certain circumstances. This fact, in the meantime, indicates that tolerance of meat is not the ultimate instruction of Buddha but merely an expediency. In the sixth century, a famous Chinese Buddhist Shen Yue wrote an article entitled "On Ultimate Compassion" in which he put forward that the Buddha "set up the saying of three-net-meat" only to "adopt an expediency." Not until Mahayana sutras such as the *Nirvana Sutra* appeared was the ban on meat formally issued and the earlier and more convenient way of meat-eating was clearly abandoned. The teaching of Mahayana Buddhism embodies the complete and ultimate instruction of the Buddha.

This interpretation does not lack canonical basis. As a matter of fact, there emerged a formal ban on "three-net-meat" in

India after some Mahayana sutras were publicized. It was proposed that "the tolerance of the three-net-meat serves to gradually prohibit it." This means that the Buddha's instruction of vegetarianism underwent a change from the expediency of Theravada teaching (allowing the three-net-meat) to the promotion of vegetarianism in Mahayana Buddhism. With respect to the Buddhist precept of eating a meat-free diet, the advocacy of vegetarianism in Chinese Buddhism is the peak of Mahayana Buddhism.

In the sixth century, China officially endorsed vegetarianism as the precept by which all Buddhist monks and nuns must abide. This also had a profound impact on the secular life of Chinese society. Thus, the ban on killing animals for food in Chinese Buddhism not only triggered the fashion of vegetarianism within Buddhist temples and monasteries, but also affected other regulations in daily life and was related to a more comprehensive ban on meat. For instance, the empire extended the comprehensive ban on meat from the circle of Buddhists to a realm beyond Buddhism, such as the requirement of substituting fruits and vegetables for meat in sacred offerings and in many secular activities.

Meanwhile a series of measures were taken by the government, such as a prohibition of hunting and a ban on leather (wearing animal products.) Apart from the requirement of a vegetarian diet for Buddhists, aspects of Buddhist culture have inspired folk life and still flourish today. For example, there are the folk customs of observing vegetarianism for every breakfast, and adhering to a vegetarian diet six days per month (the 8th, the 14th, the 15th, the 23rd and the last two days of the Chinese lunar month). It can be said that from the sixth century onwards, the campaign related to vegetarianism gradually developed into a kind of cultural habit and became part of the ethical code throughout China, through the operation of national political and cultural influence. Despite the fact that vegetarianism is mostly regarded in China as a sort of life education that is closely related to the Buddhist tradition, it should be noted that vegetarianism is not only a Buddhist commandment, but also more importantly, that it helps humanity develop compassion and encourages the cultivation of human awareness.

# Buddhism:
# The Hidden Thread

WILL TUTTLE

## *Bodhi* and *Karuna*: Individual and Community

The Buddhist teachings emphasize cultivating the two fundamental powers in our human world: the power of the individual and that of the community. Similarly, two primary ideas in Buddhism are *bodhi*, the awakened wisdom that is our true nature, and *karuna*, compassion, the expression and cultivation of this wisdom in our lives, expressed as *ahimsa*, nonharmfulness toward others. Through our individual efforts and practice we can purify our body, speech, and mind and awaken bodhi within us, freeing ourselves from the delusion of essential separateness. This awakening brings individual liberation from suffering and delusion, and compassion for those in our community. Awakening is seen as the goal and purpose of our individual human life, and is supported by and inseparable from our sangha, the community with whom we share our life. In the narrow sense, *sangha* is the community of fellow Buddhist aspirants, and in a broader sense, it is the community of all living beings.

Vegan living is similarly based on cultivating both individual and community wisdom, leading to compassion for each other and for all beings. The word vegan was coined in 1944 by Donald Watson with the purpose of accounting for motivation (ignored by the word vegetarian) and extending our ethical concern to every aspect of our relations with animals. The definition of the word as adopted by the Vegan Society reads, "Veganism is a philosophy and way of living which seeks to exclude, as far as possible and practicable, all forms of exploitation of, and cruelty to, animals, for food, clothing, or any other purpose..." It's clear that veganism and Buddhism share a similar basic motivation and orientation to encourage respect and kindness in both individuals and in our communities, and to extend this respect to all who are sentient, i.e., capable of suffering.

**The Power of Community**
Veganism and all traditions of Buddhism fundamentally agree that animals are ethically relevant, and that we are called to transform ourselves and our communities so that we treat each other, and animals, with kindness and respect. Significantly, one thing we all understand is that the only reason any of us buys and eats animal flesh, cow's milk products, and eggs, as well as products such as leather, fur, and wool, and attends rodeos, zoos, and so forth, is because of the communities in which we are raised and educated. The behavior, as well as the supporting narrative, of

eating and abusing animals on a daily basis, is injected into virtually all of us from infancy without our permission by well-meaning parents, teachers, relatives, doctors, and priests, as well as by a continuous stream of corporate and government messaging.

It is clear that eating animal foods causes terrible (and unnecessary) suffering to animals, and it's also clear that we are not doing this out of a free choice but because we are conditioned to do so by our communities. We follow orders that were, and continue to be, ritually inserted into our consciousness by people we trusted implicitly from our pre-verbal past. Questioning such deeply-rooted and pervasive orders is no easy task because we identify profoundly with the "tribe" that gave us our language and made our life possible. Our tribal community today has compelled us all to participate in relentless daily food rituals that reduce animals to exploitable, expendable commodities. This cultural program of animal agriculture installed in all of us by our communities is an invisible "deep state" that operates in the shadows and propels humanity's unremitting violence against animals that is now estimated to be killing about sixty thousand animals globally every second for food.[1]

Buddhism, like any authentic spiritual tradition, is profoundly inimical to this violent system into which we've all been born. Its core teachings emphasize cultivating universal compassion for all beings, explicitly including animals, urging mindfulness and encouraging us to vigilantly question the internal narratives that drive our emotions and actions. The essential practice is cultivating awareness, and liberating our minds from toxic cultural indoctrination, and discovering the freedom and inner peace of our true nature. In actual fact, Buddhism has been a potent healing force in the world, helping liberate both individuals and societies from eating animal foods and from abusing animals as commodities in general. My own case is a good example.

I was born in Massachusetts in the early 1950s and, like virtually all of us, was brought up in a family that ate the typical diet emphasizing meat, diary products, and eggs. I never questioned it because vegetarianism was unheard of and protein, calcium, and human superiority narratives were relentlessly injected into my consciousness with every meal by everyone in my world. No alternative was conceivable.

When I went away to college, I started to question the violence of the Vietnam War and the exploitative nature of capitalism. I also discovered books on Zen, yoga, and other Eastern philosophies, practices that were intriguing and inspiring, although they did not prompt any dietary questioning. After graduation, I embarked with my younger brother on what we felt was a spiritual pilgrimage, practicing meditation and walking, without money, for quite a few months, heading west and then south on the little back-country roads that led us eventually to a Zen center in Alabama.

It was 1975. While walking through Tennessee, we stopped for a few weeks at a community called The Farm, which was the largest hippie commune in the world with about 900 people living there. They called themselves vegetarians but were actually practicing what we would call veganism today (a virtually unknown word then). They didn't eat meat, fish, dairy, eggs, or honey, and many even avoided leather and other animal-sourced products. Their motivation was based on ethical concerns about the abuse of animals used in the animal agriculture industry, the suffering of hungry people, and the violence of war. They told me they were eating lower on the food chain so there would be enough food for everyone to eat, explaining the inherent wastefulness of feeding grains to animals, and that the injustice of food shortages worldwide was a primary underlying cause of human conflict. Their inspiring example, and participating with them in eating daily plant-based meals together, transformed my food orientation and I have not eaten meat since. About five years later, in 1980, after learning more about the routine abuse of hens for eggs and cows for dairy products, in addition to the devastating impact of human exploitation of animals in general, I became a vegan.

What is clear to me is that this fortuitous transition to vegan living was due not just to my individual yearning, questioning, and efforts, but also to the positive influence and example of the community at The Farm, and the other Buddhist *sanghas* I've lived in. The Farm was not a Buddhist community on the outside, but I realized with time that in many ways, it was. The Farm's leader and spiritual teacher, Stephen Gaskin, had originally started the community that eventually became The Farm in Tennessee by offering his "Monday Night Class" in San Francisco, which inspired hundreds of young people to convert old school busses and go on the road together in search of land where they could co-create a community to put his teachings into action.

Stephen considered himself a student of Suzuki Roshi, founder of the San Francisco Zen Center. When I was at The Farm in 1975, Suzuki Roshi's book, *Zen Mind, Beginners Mind*, had just been released and was the most popular book among the residents. It was widely discussed and embraced by the community. The Farm's vegan orientation was a manifestation of its willingness to question many of the dominant cultural narratives surrounding gender roles, food, livelihood, meditation, birthing practices, consumerism, and war, and it did so from the framework of a Buddhist orientation emphasizing personal responsibility, compassion, regular meditation, and cultivating awareness and respect for animals, ecosystems, and other people. Later, I lived and practiced in Zen and Vajrayana Buddhist meditation centers in Huntsville, Atlanta, and the San Francisco Bay Area, all of which were vegetarian. These living situations taught me about and deepened my commitment to practicing nonviolence and cultivating compassion for other living beings.

In 1984, when I went to South Korea and lived as a Zen monk at Songgwangsa Buddhist temple, I found myself in a spiritual community that had been practicing vegan living since the thirteenth century: no meat, dairy, eggs, wool, silk, leather, or any killing of mosquitoes and other insects. It was obvious to me that this practice of mindful consumption and action—striving to practice *ahimsa* as the fundamental guiding ethical light—was both a result of centuries of cultural spiritual wisdom, and also the basis for the propagation and continuation of this wisdom into the future.

We were practicing sitting meditation for about twelve hours daily, and as the weeks and months passed, it became clearer that any action that harms others tends to destabilize the mind, disrupt inner stillness, and impede progress in meditation. Refraining from manipulating, exploiting, deceiving, and harming others, including both humans and animals, and striving to treat them with kindness and respect, not only helps them be happy and free, but also brings happiness and freedom to myself, and co-creates a culture of respect, equality, and justice.

I grew to understand more deeply the importance of the precepts, which serve as guides to ethical conduct. Just as our consciousness affects our behavior, so also, our behavior affects our consciousness and indeed, our consciousness can never rise higher than the level of our behavior. Eating animal foods places an unrecognized and invisible ceiling on our spiritual capacities, desensitizing and disturbing us both physically and mentally, spiritually and ethically. Though I'd already been a vegan for a few years when I went to Songgwangsa, I felt that living there nourished the roots of vegan living, helping them reach more deeply into my heart.

Since then, continuing with Buddhist meditation practice and study for the past forty years, there's a clear sense of the profound degree to which our minds are colonized by our cultural upbringing. In inner stillness and receptivity, the eternal, sky-like nature of the mind may become apparent, giving rise to luminous joy. Released from the prison of deluded self-oriented ambition, craving, and fear, the mind rests in wholeness, no longer essentially separate from the world it perceives. For virtually all of us, this basic wisdom is repressed and covered over by the culture into which we are born, a culture that colonizes our minds and compels us to relentlessly eat animals. This cultural programming wounds our awareness and sensitivity, hijacks our thoughts and actions, and leaves us spiritually lost, herded into a societal mentality and lifestyle based on competition, manipulation, and disconnectedness from animals, nature, and ourselves. Though covered over by clouds, thick smoke, and fog, our minds are essentially undamageable, like the infinite sky, clear, bright, and eternally unhindered by the fleeting clouds of human experience. Wisdom teachings can be rays of light that reveal and thus bringing healing.

It hasn't been difficult to see that the same basic truths shining through the Buddhist teachings also illuminate teachings of many other traditions, including Christian, Sufi, Jewish, Jain, Hindu, Taoist, Confucian, and others. The underlying wisdom is similar: to connect authentically with the deeper level of our mind, and to be loving and respectful in our relations with others. In Buddhism, we are told that we are called to leave home in order to walk the path of awakening, and metaphorically this points in the same direction: to question the official narratives that have infected our minds and that compel us to slavishly collude with a system that is devastating every dimension of our individual and collective health. There seem to be three basic steps:

1. Make efforts to question and free ourselves internally from the existing cultural framework;
2. practice meditation, mindfulness, and introspection to develop our capacity to understand directly the unimpeded freedom, compassion, and harmony of our essential nature;

3. co-create and support communities that foster this liberation and respect, to help our entire culture be positively transformed.

These three steps continually loop back and reinforce each other.

## The Hidden Thread

The Buddhist teachings, like all authentic spiritual teachings, are potent and effective in their capacity to heal and liberate because they insist that we devote ourselves unflaggingly to mindfulness and self-inquiry on every level, including our relationships, emotions, behaviors, and purchases. I now realize that it was the Buddhist teaching of non-harmfulness that was shining through the vibrant example of vegan living that I walked into on The Farm and that ended forever my consumption of animal flesh. Living in Buddhist centers and practicing and studying the Dharma teachings have deepened this transformation and have also led to creating books, essays, trainings, workshops, and presentations that have helped people of diverse backgrounds transition to vegan living. These people, in turn, have gone on to create films, classes, study groups, sanctuaries, conferences, and other innovative means of sharing the vegan message, reaching even more people who similarly share and contribute to the awakening of humanity and the promotion of the vegan message. The hidden thread in all this is the underlying Buddhist teaching of questioning narratives and cultivating awareness and respect.

It's well understood that the awakening experienced by the Buddha 2,600 years ago in northern India helped transform Indian society away from animal sacrifice and meat-eating, and toward the vegetarianism for which India has been renowned for the past two millennia. Because of the continuous efforts of innumerable people in every generation for the next roughly 130 generations until today, this thread of including animals in our sphere of moral concern has not been lost, and continues to bring healing and awakening to our world. Visiting China, Taiwan, Korea, Vietnam, and many Buddhist centers in the west, I've seen that vegan living is mandated and encouraged for both monastics and lay Buddhists as an integral part of the Dharma teachings in many lineages and traditions. Its beneficial effect on the wider society is incalculable.

Just as I was transformed by the Mahayana Buddhist-inspired communities, The Farm and Songgwangsa, and just as others have been transformed by reading *The World Peace Diet*, and have gone on to help transform others who will transform others, so also Thoreau, Emerson, and Alcott in my hometown of Concord, Massachusetts, were transformed by their pioneering discovery of Buddhist texts. The Concord Transcendalists created one of the first western communal experiments in vegan living, "Fruitlands," in the mid-nineteenth century, and went on to inspire countless more people with their writings and example. The same hidden thread continues to wend its way through our culture today. If we look deeply enough into the ethical foundations for vegan living, their sources, and their sources' sources, we usually find threads leading back sooner or later to Buddhist teachings.

Already, in the first century BCE, Buddhist monks had travelled far from India, bringing the Dharma teachings to western Asia, Greece, and as far as the British Isles. There have been surprising levels of global cross-fertilization of ideas over the millennia. Even in more recent times, we can see this interconnectedness, for example, in how Buddhist and Asian spiritual ideas influenced Thoreau and the other Transcendentalists, who influenced Tolstoy, who influenced Gandhi, who influenced Martin Luther King and Thich Nhat Hanh, who further influenced many more. This is but a tiny glimpse into a vast web of influences that unite humanity and demonstrate how, as individuals, we are both the products, as well as the creators, of communities and societies, and the web of relationships that underlie them.

We cannot say that the Buddha's teachings of vegetarianism and veganism are the only source. It is likely that he was one of several, perhaps many, voices that helped usher in vegetarian living in India during the Axial Age and subsequently into the yogic and other spiritual and cultural traditions of the Indian subcontinent. Mahavir, the great sage of the Jain tradition who lived concurrently with the Buddha, is certainly another force, as were their contemporaries, Confucius and Laozi in China and Pythagoras in the eastern Mediterranean, all planting seeds of *ahimsa* and perhaps carrying them forward from much more ancient traditions that have been lost to us today.

The essential point is that the Buddhist teachings, like all spiritual teachings, can only be understood when lived and practiced, and that our generation, like every generation, is called to re-create the teachings in order to pass them on and to discover them anew in the uniqueness of our present circumstances. For example, there is the ancient Japanese Buddhist teaching of *shojin* that is being rediscovered by people today. Shojin is "religious abstention from animal foods" and is based on the core teaching of *ahimsa*, and is understood to support *samadhi*. *Samadhi* is deep meditative stillness in which the mind transcends its usual conflicted, anxious, and busy condition, quiets down, and becomes clear, bright, free, and serenely poised in the present moment. *Shojin* and *samadhi* are seen to work together, with *shojin* purifying the body-mind and allowing, though certainly not guaranteeing, access to the spiritually enriching experience of *samadhi*.

Entering the inner stillness of *samadhi* typically entails a lot of practice, patiently returning our attention to the present moment, and requires that our mind be undisturbed by our outer actions. This is why the spirit of *ahimsa* that inspires *shojin* is important. The spirit of *shojin* is compassion and sees animals as sentient subjects rather than mere commodities. The practice of *shojin* liberates us from both outer actions that are harmful, as well as inner mental states that accompany eating animal foods. These mental states—agitation, fear, panic, despair, sadness, aggressiveness, disconnectedness, despair, and dullness—are virtually unavoidable if we are buying and eating animal-sourced foods, brought into us as vibrational frequencies with the foods we are eating, generated within us by our own undeniably abusive food choices and the psychological blocking these actions demand. These negative mental states tend to reduce our capacity to meditate effectively and hinder our ability to reach higher levels of spiritual illumination.

It's sometimes said that there are three pillars to Buddhist practice and awakening: *sila* (ethical living), *samadhi*, and *prajna* (wisdom). Like a three-legged stool, all three are equally necessary and support each other. *Sila*, mindfulness of the precepts and careful practice of kindness in our relations with others, is the spirit of veganism and *shojin*. This creates the foundation for *samadhi*, the stillness and serenity of mind that lies at the heart of spiritual life. *Samadhi* leads to *prajna*, the liberating wisdom that represents the full flowering of human awareness, dissolving the old wall of delusion and bringing liberation, understanding, and compassion. Both *samadhi* and *prajna* support *sila* in an organic way, because the awakening that Buddhism aims for is realizing the essential interconnectedness of all life, which naturally and joyfully propels us to act with sensitivity and respect toward other expressions of life. Vegan living is an essential element of this virtuous circle. Without it, the circle becomes vicious. Causing and eating violence leads to desensitization, which leads to further abuse, disconnectedness, delusion, and suffering.

## The Enlightenment Fallacy

Outer compassion and inner stillness feed each other. Veganism and ethical living are essential to our spiritual health because they remove a fundamental hindrance on our individual path and help create harmony in our community. For this reason, there's an old

Buddhist saying attributed to Padmasambhava, "Though the view should be as vast as the sky, keep your conduct as fine as barley flour." This essential teaching emphasizing vegan values of caring and kindness is an important healing antidote to a damaging delusion common in many Buddhist, yoga, and other spiritual and progressive communities. We can call this delusion the "enlightenment fallacy" because it arises as a false sense of individual license to do as we like because we believe we are spiritually advanced.

This enlightenment fallacy reinforces and activates the basic sense of entitlement and arrogance that is inserted into all of us as products of a culture organized at its living core around the shared ritual of eating foods sourced from animals whom we collectively dominate and exploit. This violence is well understood today to be completely unnecessary and counter-productive to our physical, cultural and environmental health. However, the enlightenment fallacy attempts to justify this by "spiritualizing" our disconnectedness, denial, and daily contribution to violence through propagating what seems to be a more lofty and enlightened perspective. This fashionable perspective clouds our awareness and convinces us that our behavior of buying and eating animal-sourced foods is either not relevant to our spiritual practice, or that it is actually an indication of our spiritual attainments. There are several versions of this enlightenment fallacy.

One is that because of our spiritual attainment, we are now free of attachments and judgments. We are no longer trapped in the net of discrimination, this fallacy affirms, and are therefore free to eat anything we like. We see that everything has "one taste" and so now that we have discovered this and have freed ourselves from the discriminating mind, we can live our lives free from the rules that are only meant for those who are less accomplished. Another version is that because we are more enlightened, we now realize that the whole phenomenal world is but *maya*, an illusion, and therefore no animals are really killed, and in fact nothing negative ever really happens. Love is the only power, and so we can eat our hot dogs with love and understanding and no harm is done. This narrative assures us that we either transform the negativity with our high vibration, or that we are so awake that we realize that the animals we're eating are illusory, as is all pain and suffering, so it doesn't matter what we do in the outer world. All that matters is the quality of our consciousness.

A similar narrative is that we may have attained the "karma-less" state, where we are free from karma, duality and consequences. We realize there is no essential self, and no world, and we are thus free to do as we like. We are no longer bound by conventional morality, which is a system of rules that is artificial and imprisons us in delusions of "good" and "evil." Now we are free of this confining dualism, the narrative goes, and we can act as we please. There is a saying by Augustine that points in this direction, "Love God and do as you will, and all is well." Many Buddhists and other spiritual practitioners follow a similarly tempting rationalization as well, proclaiming that spiritual illumination is liberation from dualism and rules, and they are free to do as their "heart" tells them, or to eat the foods to which their "body" guides them. They love the animals they eat. They are blessing them and helping them to have a more evolved rebirth. Or even better, they see that it's all just a play of illusion and that the One Light is always shining, no matter what is happening in the outer world.

Padmasambhava's wisdom (and there are many other examples of this wisdom in the Buddhist teachings) specifically addresses the devastating fallacy in these hubristic narratives. When our view is as vast, deep, bright, and all-encompassing as the sky, then we keep our conduct as fine as flour. It's precisely because our view is vast that we are more sensitive to the consequences of actions, and take them seriously. We experience the infinite interconnectedness of all manifestations of life, and our heart is naturally bursting with compassion for others, even as we see they are not "others" at all, but essentially inseparable from us. This realization is the foundation of authentic morality, kindness, spiritual awakening, and of all the precepts. We naturally delight in helping and blessing others as best we can, and recoil from actions that exploit or abuse others for our own advantage.

We should be suspicious of any narrative that allows or encourages harming or using others because of seeing they are not separate, or seeing they are eternal and undamageable, and so forth. Clinging to either duality or non-duality is still clinging. There are many aspects to the enlightenment fallacy, and the various rationalization narratives are all the more insidious because of the armor they bestow, hardening hearts and conveying a toxic pseudo-spirituality that harms not just the animals but everyone in any way touched by these delusions and their resulting behaviors. While it certainly may be helpful and healing to practice viewing the pain and loss that we personally experience as transient and illusory, it is the height of delusion to discount the pain and loss we inflict on others by rationalizing it as being transient and illusory. We may often add further layers to the narrative, for example that it's just for their own good, or it's just their *karma*, or that we're just not attached to outer forms, or that we're just reflecting back to them their own violence. The "just" in all these narrative excuses is the just of justification.

To the degree we are wounded and abused as children, we tend to grow into adults who are unfortunately propelled to likewise inflict abuse on others. As products of a technocratic herding culture, we are all harmed from infancy in countless ways, and our woundedness can erode our capacity to be mindful of our conduct, and sensitive to our inner wisdom and to others. The Buddhist teachings call us to heal, to look deeply and mindfully, and to question the fundamental narrative of the herding culture into which we've all been born. This herding narrative that reduces beings to commodities is the utter antithesis of both *bodhi* and *karuna*, wisdom and compassion, the prime teachings of Buddhism that free us as individuals, and create the foundation of communities where harmony, joy, equality, and abundance are possible for all.

Awakening from the desensitizing stupor inflicted on us from infancy by the herding culture that exploits not just animals and ecosystems but us humans as well is a monumental effort. It calls us to question virtually all of our inner narratives, explanations, and stories, and to cultivate our capacity for inner silence so that we can be guided in our life in a way that is free from this harmful conditioning. In receptive awareness we find that intuitive insight emerges, and this can be seen as the foundation of the wisdom and compassion that are at the heart of the Buddhist dharma.

The transformative insight that the historical Buddha experienced and shared as best he could is a direct understanding of the deeper truth of our nature, bringing peace, joy, and freedom. It is insight into the cause of suffering in the delusion of essential separateness, which compels us to try endlessly to get what we want and keep away what we don't want, and to see others as instruments in this miserable struggle. This is samsara, the suffering that never ends in countless lifetimes until we awaken our heart and mind and realize that we are all waves on the same ocean. This awakening and teaching, the hidden thread that has brought healing through the ages, is available to each and every one of us now. May we give thanks every day for another opportunity to awaken, and to contribute to our community, and to cultivate our mind and heart so that our view becomes as vast as the sky and our conduct as fine as barley flour.

**References:**
1.   This number is arrived at by simple division of the 75 billion land animals and two trillion marine animals conservatively estimated to be killed annually for food.

# Engaged Veganism and Interbeing with Other Animals:

## Mindful Consumption as Practice for Liberation

MARION ACHOULIAS

My karmic entanglement with other animals has no beginning and from where I stand at this moment, I do not see an end. It started when I was an embryo in my mother's body and was exposed to traces of animal products, not to mention tar and lead from her cigarettes.

I have struggled with the pain of knowing about the ongoing injustices of slaughterhouses and vivisection laboratories throughout my adulthood. At times, I have refused to acknowledge it, and at other times I have managed to suppress my horror and somehow get myself to act. I became a vegan, wrote letters to companies, volunteered for animal refuges, and attended and organized outreach events. Bouts of action were punctuated with long periods of despair in which I succumbed to hopelessness and self-pity that I should have been born into such a mad world.

My life has been fragmented by my struggle with the reality of unspeakable cruelty and I wish for it to become whole. I am ready now to look into my own suffering and the ways in which it is connected to the suffering of others, both nonhuman and human. Animal suffering is still part of my deep consciousness, partly because I ate animal products for so long. Anger is still in me as I continue to live and participate in a society built on injustice. It has been painful to realize that even though I am involved in social justice work and eat a plant-based diet, I am nevertheless entangled in the same causes and conditions that give rise to exploitation and violence. But how could it be any different? I am only at the beginning of a true vegan awakening.

Thich Nhat Hanh developed socially engaged Buddhism in times of war. He decided to take his spiritual practice out of the monastery and into the world to help relieve the suffering he witnessed around him in his home country of Vietnam. Decades later in the West, in the midst of the suffering caused by carnist consumer culture,[1] the Zen master and peace activist is showing us the path to healing and peace[2] in his contemporary interpretation of a key classical Buddhist teaching on the consumption of the four main nutriments or fuels, namely edible foods, sense impressions, volition/intention, and consciousness. The original text teaches that each mental state and all phenomena can only manifest if we continuously feed them.[3]

In the first part of this essay, I present Thich Nhat Hanh's teachings on veganism as wholesome nutriment. I will then briefly describe the ways in which I apply the principle of the four fuels to my experience as a vegan who believes in the multidimensionality of vegan mindfulness practice. Engaged veganism is a vast dharmic door for liberation based on the understanding that it will enable uncountable beings both human and nonhuman to dramatically reduce suffering and to live fulfilling lives. It is a perspective that addresses social, psychological, and environmental problems from a radically inclusive perspective. We are karmically intertwined with all species, and yet we are just recently becoming aware of the great extent to which the consumption of animal-sourced foods affects us all.

## The Fuel of Edible Food

Transformation begins the moment we become aware of the elements we allow to enter our body and mind. What am I eating? Is it some-thing or is it some-one? Are we feeding joy or harm in ourselves or others? To wake us up, Thich Nhat Hanh uses strong words: "Eating meat and drinking alcohol with mindfulness, we will realize that we are eating the flesh of our own children; we are eating our own planet earth," he writes in his influential *Blue Cliff Letter* from 2006.[4]

Note that his definition of vegetarianism includes the avoidance of dairy and egg products, "because they are products of the meat industry. If we stop consuming, they will stop producing. Only collective awakening can create enough determination for action."[5] Nhat Hanh further announced that all retreats and practice centres of his Plum Village tradition in Asia, Europe, and North America from then on will only serve plant based meals and he "trusts that lay practitioners will understand and support this decision wholeheartedly. We know that if there is no collective awakening, then the earth and all species will not have a chance to be saved. Our daily life has to show that we are awake."[6] Already five years prior, in the fateful year of 2001, the spiritual leader recognized that mindful consumption is the primary way we have of "preventing violence to penetrate and grow in our body and consciousness."[7] During a public talk at the University of Massachusetts, he described in detail the suffering of chickens languishing in battery cages with the warning that the ingestion of the products of such agony means swallowing the animals' frustration and despair. A daily diet of misery must leave its traces, especially if we believe, as many Buddhists (and some scientists) do, that consciousness is not confined to the brain but that all information is contained in each cell of our body.[8] With each bite of food—the building blocks of our body-mind complex—we are connecting deeply to the causes and conditions that produce the things we take in, digest, and absorb. We cannot escape their effects.

Buddhist psychology gives us the tools to confront our habits of denial and the tendency to rationalize our often quite irrational actions post facto. Studies show consistently that behaviour determines thought, rather than the other way around.[9] While we are caught in habitual patterns, we are not free to clearly see their implications. The more animal products we eat, the more we will feel the need to justify this choice, and the more we distance ourselves emotionally from the victims of our food preferences. This vicious cycle cuts us off from the world and makes it increasingly difficult for us to be in touch with other living beings in the world. Hence the Buddha advised us to eat in such a way that allows compassion to be possible.[10] Maybe not surprisingly, it was only when I decided to become vegan that I found the courage to watch undercover footage of animal slaughter.

For me, going vegan has also meant consuming in a way that makes honesty possible. Or, in Nhat Hanh's words, eating mindfully means "to only eat what does not make a war in your body and your mind."[11] He says, "If you eat meat it is as if you eat your son's flesh." This acknowledges that eating mammals, fish, and birds comes much closer to cannibalism than plant eating. In addition, the use of animal products hurts other people and the environment in ways that a plant based diet does not. The Middle Way of living well, while reducing violence, is veganism.

But how is it even conceivable that we look at a fellow sentient being and see food? What is the mechanism of reducing animals to the category of killable? Eating animals impoverishes us and deadens our world because it cuts us off from the richness of life in its many diverse embodiments. Meditating on our ingrained habit energies fed through consciousness, volition and sense contact may shed light on the ways craving, fear and other negative mental formations can distort our perception of the other. Due to lack of mindful consumption, we feed a cut-throat mentality, and from its manifold manifestations grow seeds of despair that can blind us to the kindness and respect that are also always available and present.

**The Fuel of Consciousness**
According to the Yogacara tradition, our store consciousness holds all human potential for anger, fear, compassion, and transformation in the form of seeds that push us to react to internal and external triggers.[12] These seeds are not only shaped by our actions, perceptions, and experiences but also by those of many generations of predecessors along with those of countless individuals who are alive today.[13] The circumstances of historical events, institutions, and the natural environment further complicate the feedback system of consciousness. Perfect free will is an illusion, because our thoughts, inclinations, and actions are not ours alone. They are manifestations that have their origins in the seeds planted by many factors, from personal upbringing to society to global history.

Reflecting on the store consciousness's collective and interdependent nature exposes the obstacles to the transformation of our carnist culture and helps us understand why we might continue to be affected by its repercussions even though we made the life- and world-changing decision to stop contributing to animal killing directly. Across many generations, our ancestors grew increasingly alienated from the rest of nature, founding much of our economy and cultural practices on the backs of animals.

Our laws, language, and lifeways reflect and further reinforce this disconnection. It is likely that the global history of animal exploitation has left deep marks on our bodies and minds. The causes and conditions that brought us mass slaughter and factory farms, the technology and mindset of greed, the objectification of living beings, and the relentless time pressure of the kill floor pervade the foundations of our society.

Considering the increase of crime, alcohol use and domestic violence in communities near slaughterhouses,[14] we can see that the suffering of the workers who spend their days in blood and gore affect us too, even if indirectly. I often feel tempted to blame and shame those involved in the meat industry for their immorality, but I'm thereby perpetuating an already harsh and judgmental culture. If my wish is to contribute to deep transformation at a societal level, it is vital to help create conditions for open and respectful dialogue. We need spaces where we can feel safe enough to be vulnerable, to reflect on our choices honestly and to find the strength to admit when it is time for a change. Vegan advocacy that is compassionately engaged with the world in all its complexity can achieve this goal.

Thich Nhat Hanh even advocates compassion for the "worst" criminals, saying that if we had to live through their upbringing and conditions, we would probably be in their place today. The realization that we are not that different from our "opponents" in a debate, that we all share the same seeds and potential for love and hate, makes connection across differences possible. The objective reality of violence and cruelty that we perceive as existing outside of us is *itself* a creation of our collective consciousness. For a collective vegan awakening, we are called to consider our own role in creating the conditions for animal exploitation as one of many symptoms of the confused and materialistic society in which we are participating, whether we want to or not. This is the practice of examining the interdependent co-arising nature of our consciousness, and conjointly, our necessary involvement as a participatory factor in the arising of phenomena in the world, even of those events that seem to have "nothing to do with me." This is the practice of *Paratantra*.[15]

Just as the collective is in the individual, the individual also influences the collective.[16] The moment we think, speak, or act with kindness and respect, the world changes. Modern veganism is here because slaughterhouses and factory farms are here. As the violence reaches ever more extreme levels, the vegan response represents our awakening to compassion and radical inclusiveness.

### The Fuel of Intention

Intention, or directionality of mind,[17] is a powerful source of energy, and indeed is the decisive factor involved in the creation of karma because it determines the moral quality of an act. Intention energy draws on the seeds of respect, kindness, anger, and craving in our store consciousness. As a practitioner and activist, I try to consciously set positive and benevolent intentions because they have the power to align my behaviour, thought, and speech with my purpose. Often, however, I see that less than pure impulses slip in, even though I may not be aware of this right away. In one instance, for example, I realized that when I decided to stop buying dairy products, my intentions were not unified but rather quite conflicted. While my main motivation was compassion for the calves, I could sense an underlying itch to punish those "evil" companies that exploit animals. I also noticed that this punitive attitude added a slightly shrill tone to my voice for a while. To stop wasting precious energy on unnecessary inner struggle, I now practice letting go of any intentions (subtle and gross) that could diminish or compromise the work of peace that the abolition of animal exploitation signifies. I meditate regularly to help catch those seeds in my consciousness before they manifest as guilt, antagonism, fear, or the craving for recognition.

Intention is so powerful that it also colors perception. If craving for a steak overpowers our positive intentions, we are at risk of distorting the reality of interbeing. We will *forget* the fact that we are about to sink our teeth into a body part of a sentient being who wanted to live, just as we want to live. Our appetite and habit energy may be pushing us to reduce the animal to the status of a thing, of mere food to be eaten.[18] Only in rare cases is it malevolent intent that motivates people to eat meat, wear fur, or even to work in a slaughterhouse. Their deepest desire for kindness is typically buried under many layers of conflict, distractions, and craving. Therefore, the best way to serve people involved in harmful action is to help them become clear about their intentions and deepest desires, and to remind them that yes, alternative ways of living exist. "We should talk to them in such a way that touches their hearts," says Thich Nhat Hanh, "that helps them to engage on the path that will bring them true happiness; the path of love and understanding, the courage to let go. When they have tasted a little bit of peace and love, they may wake up."[19]

## The Fuel of Sense Contact

The eyes, ears, nose, skin, and mind are our sense doors to truth but too often they are a source of inner chaos. When a sight or sound triggers the potentialities of craving or aversion in our store consciousness, we may feel compelled to do something un-called for, even if this thought or act goes against our vision of the good. We can always try to simply supress the impulse, which is probably what we have been trained to do since childhood. This strategy, however, costs energy, which eventually depletes us, especially if we try to deny indignation and sadness in situations where we have witnessed or experienced unkindness or injustice. To learn to respond appropriately in situations, I've found it helpful to protect myself from unwholesome input for a certain time. Many challenges, though, cannot, and should not, be avoided. In either case, it helps my sanity to be mindful of the fact that I will probably need some time for rest and reflection after particularly trying situations.

In the Buddha's discourse on the causation of suffering,[20] sense contact with the world is symbolized by a "slayed cow" who, having lost her protective skin, is exposed to the elements unguarded. Without the filter of mindfulness, we suffer like that cow; sense stimulation can overwhelm us and parasitically feed on our life energy. Fatigue, anxiety, and a deep-seated sense of apprehension are contemporary symptoms of unguarded exposure to sense stimulation. Besides social media and advertising as major culprits, getting wrapped up in certain unneeded conversations can be similarly destabilizing, even if we downplay the sometimes subtle effects, like feeling empty somehow after a negative exchange, or disheartened. I now understand that when I hear sarcasm, feelings of unease will arise in me. Yet, having been indoctrinated with unrealistic notions of autonomy and independence since childhood, I underestimate the often surprising extent to which I can either be left nourished or weakened by influences that reach me via my eyes and ears. Recently, I have started to protect myself better in difficult social situations by practicing conscious breathing to protect my inner calm, and sometimes I will excuse myself politely when necessary. I also make an effort to practice mindfulness in conversations about veganism. My hope is that these exchanges water seeds of insight, hope, and openness and do not leave the other feeling judged or depleted.

Another toxic type of conversation I wish to avoid is one I have with myself. At times, so much as the mere sight of meat on a plate or a fur collar can cause a pinch of aversion and condemnation to manifest in me, bogging me down in an internal dispute. What a waste of energy! The alternative is to select my object of concentration and attention by remembering that "the path of liberation for all beings is larger than this. I am not helping a single animal by drowning in negative thoughts." But this clarity of mind does not appear by way of sheer willpower. Only when I "give myself a break" from time to time can I heal, get stronger and cope better with the fact that we are surrounded by unrelenting evidence of animal suffering. While noxious sense stimulation can chip away at my vitality, I know that being in contact with wholesome elements supports me on the practice path. Thich Nhat Hanh reminds us that whatever the situation, nourishing elements are always available if we are in touch with the reality of the present moment. Whenever I can, I nourish my seeds of hope and strength through gratitude for the trees, the sky, the smile of a stranger, and the sweet face of a rescued animal in safety.

I feel joy when I hear that Thich Nhat Hanh's monastics of Plum Village in Thailand distribute small slips of paper kindly requesting that only plant foods be offered in their alms bowl.[21] I wonder what the Buddha would have said about such an apparent break with tradition. I trust that if the Awakened One could see our current situation of environmental devastation, world hunger perpetuated by the production of meat and dairy, and the unspeakable violence against animals, he surely would agree. And does it really matter whether or not the historical Buddha accepted meat in his alms bowl? To be honest, yes, it has bothered me quite a bit. Even so, in keeping with the Zen spirit of not allowing any tradition, doctrine, or authorities to turn into obstacles to liberation, what seems most important *is my own practice.*[22]

The human body-mind, in perpetual interaction with everything and everyone else through space and time, is truly world-creating. It is up to us to decide whether we create hell for ourselves and others or a window for peace. Even in the darkest hour, we can be a light unto ourselves and the world through our practice. I encourage you to make engaged veganism your own, live it deeply, and share the joy of this path with all sentient beings.

**References:**

1.  For more on carnism see Melanie Joy, *Why we Love Dogs, Eat Pigs, and Wear Cows: An Introduction to Carnism* (Berkeley, CA: Conari Press, 2011).
2.  For more on this idea see Will Tuttle, *The World Peace Diet: Eating for Spiritual Health and Social Harmony* (New York: Lantern Books 2005), 275.
3.  See "The Son's Flesh Sutra." Bikkhu Bodhi, trans., *The Connected Discourses of the Buddha: A New translation of the Samyutta Nikaya* (Boston: Wisdom Publications, 2000), 597–599.
4.  Thich Nhat Hanh, "Sitting in the Autumn Breeze," *Plum Village*, http://plumvillage.org/letters-from- thay/sitting-in-the-autumn-breeze/.
5.  Ibid.
6.  Ibid.
7.  Thich Nhat Hanh, *The Practice of Peace and Nonviolence in Family, School, and the Workplace*, (Dharma Talk from 16/8/2001 at Lowell, MA), https://tnhaudio.org.
8.  See International Consciousness Research Laboratories (Princeton University), https://newicrl.org/scholarly-publications.
9.  See Dan Ariely, *Predictably Irrational* (New York: Harper Perennial, 2010).
10. Thich Nhat Hanh, *Mindful Consumption* (Dharma Talk from17/7/1998 at Plum Village, France), https://sites.google.com/site/tnhdhamma/Home/test-list/mindful-consumption.
11. Ibid.
12. See D.K. Nauriyal, Michael S. Drummond and Y.B. Lal, *Buddhist Thought and Applied Psychological Research* (London & New York: Routledge).
13. Thich Nhat Hanh, *Understanding Our Mind* (Berkeley, CA: Parallax, 2006), 40.
14. E.g. Amy J. Fitzgerald, Linda Kalof, Thomas Dietz, "Slaughterhouses and Increased Crime Rates," *Organization and Environment* 22 (2009).
15. Nhat Hanh, *Understanding our Mind*, 200.
16. Nhat, Hanh, *Understanding our Mind*, 41.
17. Herbert V. Guenther & Leslie S. Kawamura, *Mind in Buddhist Psychology: A Translation of Ye-shes rgyal-mtshan's "The Necklace of Clear Understanding"* (Berkeley, CA: Dharma Publishing, 1975) Kindle Edition.
18. In the discourses on dependent co-arising, the Buddha makes clear the strong connection between suffering and clinging. Note that the Pali/Sanskrit term for clinging, *upādāna*, also means fuel. The notion of feeding and clinging is deeply connected. In the cycle of suffering, it is craving that produces the food it feeds upon. See 'Mahatanhasankhaya Sutta: The Greater Craving-Destruction Discourse' in Bikkhu Nanamoli and Bikkhu Bodhi, trans., *The Middle Length Discourses of the Buddha: A New Translation of the Majjhima Nikaya*, (Boston: Wisdom Publications, 1995), 349–361.
19. According to the Large Sutra on Perfect Wisdom, one of the key texts of the Mahayana stream, the enlightened being is "able to develop an 'honest' view on their own qualities, intentions, and motives." For an interesting introduction to Buddhist ethics, character and nature see David E. Cooper and Simon P. James, *Buddhism, Virtue, and Environment* (Hants, UK & Burlington, VT: Ashgate, 2005), 92.
20. Bodhi, trans., *The Son's Flesh Sutra*, 598.
21. Brother Chan Troi Nguyen Luc, "Almsround: The Practice of Love, Humility, and Gratitude," *Mindfulness Bell* 76 (Fall 2017), 38.
22. For more on Zen teachings on not seeking the Buddha outside oneself, encapsulated in the famous remark "Kill the Buddha!" by Zen master Lin-chi, see Lin-Chi, *The Record of Lin-chi*, Transl. by Irmgard Schloegl (Berkeley, CA: Shambala, 1976).

# Five Contemplations:
# A Mahayana Meal-time Blessing

HENG SURE

I was raised Methodist in a Midwestern Protestant Christian family. Before every family meal my parents would have us bow our heads for the meal blessing. We "said grace" around the kitchen table, with my father sitting at the head and my mother closest to the stove where the food was cooking. The "grace" that Dad spoke changed depending on the mood, the occasion, or the season. He loved poetry. Robert Burns' Scottish blessing was a favorite or, on occasion, Dad would write his own verses of blessing. Mealtime was an opportunity to hear his poetic words, fine rhyme, and rhythm in gratitude for God's creation.

Buddhists also say grace and do meal blessings, long ones, in fact. Connecting food and the spirit is a universal impulse, with gratitude being the important theme. In our Chan monasteries the mid-day meal offering lasts twenty minutes and includes prostrations to Buddhas, Bodhisattvas and Dharma Protectors. Then after sitting at the table for the meal we place our palms together, chant the names once more, and then begin the meal.

In this essay I will share a shortened version of the Five Contemplations, a portable mindfulness exercise that comes at the end of the Mahayana "grace" chants. The Five Contemplations method invites diners, while eating, to move their hearts towards humility by visualizing humanity's place in the food pyramid, to learn gratitude by growing aware of kindness received, and to become aware of the connection between the planet and the body's nutrition. This awareness has the power to turn the mundane activity of nourishing the body into a sacred contemplation.

Using these Five Contemplations with every bite, we reconnect our awareness to the source of our food. We make conscious our deepest convictions about humanity's actual place in the food chain, make an effort to stitch ourselves back into "Indra's Net," and to experience gratitude towards the Earth and all beings.

I will illustrate the major ideas with stories from a pilgrimage I took along the coast of California from 1977 to 1979. The pilgrimage involved making a full prostration to the ground every three steps, while traveling eight hundred miles up the California Coast Highway from Los Angeles to Ukiah, in Mendocino County. The journey took nearly three years and my monk companion and I traveled roughly one mile a day.

Living outdoors, walking and bowing on the highway for thirty months, and depending on people's good will offerings, my monk companion and I ate only one vegan meal per day at noon, in Buddhist monastic style. The slow pace, bowing to the ground in nature along the Pacific Coast Highway, gave me ample time to use these five perspectives to consider my actual situation as one member of the family of living beings, all of whom share an identical makeup of earth, air, fire and water.

The Five Contemplations Verse, our Buddhist "Grace," goes like this:

> This offering of the faithful is the fruit of work and care;
> I reflect upon my conduct, 'Have I truly earned my share?'
> Of the poisons in the mind the most destructive one is greed;
> As a medicine cures illness, I take only what I need
> To sustain my cultivation, and to realize the Way:
> So we contemplate with gratitude on this offering today.
> This offering of the faithful is the fruit of work and care.

Monastics receive alms-food from kind-hearted, generous donors. "The faithful" can refer to one's mother, one's wife, husband, cook, or dining hall staff. How much work went into growing, harvesting, preparing, and serving the food in my bowl that I am enjoying?

Reflecting in this way makes the nutrition of the meal go further in stimulating my gratitude. As I eat I can see my place in the larger network of life.

For example, let's say I consider the veggie dumplings, mashed potatoes with mushroom gravy, sourdough pizza bread, braised asparagus, pho soup and apple pie I'm eating today and reflect on the process that brought this delicious meal to my alms-bowl. From the farmer's effort to the purchaser, from the cook to the server, many hearts and hands participated in getting the food to my bowl. Tang Dynasty poet Li Shen captured it succinctly in "Empathy for the Farmer:"

> Beneath the blazing noonday sun, a farmer steers the plow;
> Drops of sweat fall from his body to the ground below.
> Contemplate the food you eat in your alms bowl:
> How every grain of rice comes from his bitter toil.

Being a monk makes it possible for me every day to appreciate people's generosity in supporting my life and practice. On our pilgrimage, except for the wild roadside greens we foraged, our survival depended entirely on good will offerings by people along the way.

One foggy morning more than halfway on our journey, we reached Santa Cruz, California. I came up from a bow to see a young schoolgirl, perhaps nine years old, on her bicycle. She had stopped to stare at me while I bowed and to ponder what in the world I was doing on the sidewalk in front of her house. She silently watched me take three steps and slowly bow to the ground, as I traveled past her.

I heard her ride away, and then several blocks later, I heard her bicycle approach again from the rear. She rode by and stopped and when I came up from a bow she opened her lunch box and held out a wax paper package. "Here, Mister, you better take this sandwich from my lunchbox. The way you're going, you're going to need it before you get to the corner," she said. Lunch was particularly nourishing that day.

**"I reflect upon my conduct: have I truly earned my share?"**
Mealtime provides a regular opportunity to reflect on my behavior during the day. Are my words, thoughts and deeds a gift to

my family, my team, my community or do I tend to leave behind a trail of troubles and burdens for others? Could this food I'm eating power me towards greater service and a wider circle of well-being wherever I go?

This line of the Five Contemplations verse applies in particular to monastics, to men and women who have "left the householder's life" and gone forth into the Buddha's Sangha order. We depend entirely on others' generosity for the food we eat. The food is given as free-will offerings by the laity to support the spiritual activities of the monastics who, other than their efforts to cultivate their practice, do not work to earn money for their daily bread. In principle, should the monastic reach success in his or her practice and get enlightened, the lay donor reaps the benefits of the merit that made the awakening possible.

Monastics contemplate this verse to remind them to cultivate the Way, so that they can receive the support of others without amassing a debt that they would have to repay later, perhaps in a future lifetime as a beast of burden. A verse from the tradition says expressly:

A single grain of donor's rice,
Is weighty as Sumeru [the Buddhist polar mountain], so they say.
If I should take it and then fail to cultivate,
I'll pay it back in fur and horns someday.

For members of the Sangha to accept alms, but not practice the Dharma, may create the karmic retribution of, in a future rebirth, becoming a beast of burden who must carry others' belongings to repay the debt. Contemplating according to the verse helps put the mind in a space of humility and of striving to be worthy of donors' kindnesses.

Ajahn Viradhammo, a Mahathera in the Thai forest tradition, recalls an encounter that taught him the necessity of humility when receiving alms. As a brand-new novice monk in Thailand, he was still learning how to fold his robes and carry his alms-bowl. Living outside a farming village he had to walk through rice paddies to get to the houses where the food would be offered. He recalls the awkward way he stepped along the narrow borders of the paddy fields, a pale, sun-burned Canadian monk struggling to keep his saffron robe around his body.

He saw that beneath his feet the neighboring farmer's feet were sunk knee-deep in mud and rice seedlings. The farmer was wrestling with his water buffalo and sweating beneath his cone-shaped rice-straw sun hat. He caught sight of the young monk and with full deportment and deep respect, dropped the ox's yoke, placed his palms together and made a profound half-bow to him. As the monk continued to pick his way along the paddy-field margins towards the village, he noticed the farmer secure his ox, climb out of the field, kick-start a motorbike and hurry off.

Twenty minutes later he arrived at the entrance to the village where he hoped to receive alms. He walked towards the first group of lay-people who stood waiting by their front gate. He was startled to see the same farmer from the paddy field, now with a clean shirt and combed hair, standing proudly with his wife and daughter. They were holding a silver serving bowl of steaming rice, prepared from an earlier harvest of the field he had just walked past, now cooked and ready to be offered for his meal.

Connecting the effort he had witnessed just moments before and the generosity in the smiles of the young family who stood waiting for the chance to feed him made a deep and lasting impression on Ajahn Viradhammo. He reports that this encounter sparked a resolve to always be worthy of earning his share of food offerings.

In the Thai Theravada tradition, as well as the Chinese Mahayana tradition, the monastics never say "give me" or "I want." Asking for things out of personal desire makes one a beggar, a solicitor. Mendicants have the capacity to serve as a "field of blessings" because they are practicing monastics. The mendicant says, "I am happy to make myself available, should you care to practice generosity." In this way the focus is on the resolve of the donor who wants to support the cultivator. With each offering, the donor "plants a field of blessings," which he or she harvests in the cultivation efforts, the dedications, and the prayers and chants performed by the monk or nun who receives the offerings. The layperson gives material wealth and the monastic gives back the wealth of Dharma, as indicated by the teaching, "The giving of wealth and the giving of Dharma are equal in all ways, thus completing the Perfection of Giving (*dana paramita*.)"

**"Of the poisons of the mind the most destructive one is greed."**
Greed, anger, and delusion are known as the Three Poisons, three toxic products of our minds that have the power to harm relationships, misuse resources, and foster the worst traits in humanity: insatiable craving and selfishness that can lead to corruption and injustice, violence and grief. Through the Five Contemplations, lunch becomes my place of personal transformation, by watching my thoughts and replacing the tendency towards greed with thoughts of sharing generosity and sufficiency, by replacing anger and hatred with thoughts of patience and loving-kindness, and by waking up delusion with bright awareness. World peace arrives from transcending greed and anger one thought and one bite at a time.

While bowing on the highway along the coast of California, I was pelted by the wind of passing cars and trucks. Each vehicle, zooming by at 70 miles per hour, stirred up a strong tail wind as it passed, like a wake behind a boat. In that wind tunnel, the scents and energetic atmosphere inside each vehicle wafted along in the vacuum behind it. Because freeways are places we rarely stand or walk, much less bow, few people are aware of this reality, but let me assure you that a bubble of tobacco smoke, perfume, garlic, or ripe fruit fragrances, as well as music, voices, anger and emotions float along behind for minutes after vehicles pass by, bathing any passersby in a cloud of scents, sounds and feelings. During strawberry harvest in Southern California each open-top transport truck that passed sent us to a strawberry heaven for a brief moment.

Of all the passing vehicles and their individual worlds, the most unforgettable were the livestock transport trucks, carrying cattle, sheep and pigs to feedlots, stockyards, and slaughterhouses. You may have seen those trucks, bare metal with slots on the sides to allow the animals to breathe, and a slanting bottom to allow removal of the waste. Each passing "death truck" left a cloud of scent and emotion that enveloped me for minutes as I bowed along the roadside. The feelings of fear, desperation, anger, grief and misery that poisoned the air were palpable. The smells generated by all those sensitive nervous systems jammed together in their last ride haunt me to this day.

Since meat-eating is a choice, giving life or taking life is also a choice. These fellow creatures were being subjected to this fearsome torment by choice, out of human's greed for flavor, not because of need. In the truck were living, breathing citizens of the planet, beings with mothers, children, cares and feelings. By the end of the ride they would become rump roast, sirloin, slim jims and big Macs. With each death truck that passed on the highway I vowed that I would do my utmost to help make humans more conscious, to wake everyone up to the choices we have at the dinner table, and to end the destruction caused by greed.

An antidote to greed is giving and sharing. With each meal that is free of death and cruelty, I experience gratitude for the chance to eat harmlessly. I fill my needs without participating in the economy of the death trucks. I can season my lunchtime with happiness. Replacing steak with beans may cause a brief loss of sensation for my taste buds, but, for the animal who doesn't get slaughtered, I have saved him from torment, terror, and pain.

Further, a verse by Song Dynasty poet-monk, Cloud of Vow says,

For countless years the bitter stew of hate goes boiling on;
Its enmity is ocean-deep, impossible to calm.
To learn the cause of all this killing, terror, bombs and war,
Listen to the cries at midnight, by the butcher's door.

The poet takes the issue deeper, connecting the violence generated by slaughtering animals with warfare. Butchering animals for food sparks an emotional and physical response in the bodies and minds of the sentient creatures designated as "food" by humans. That negative energy returns and seeks vengeance. Killing begets killing, and as countries mobilize their weapons, soldiers are sent to war and the cycle of violence churns on.

The suffering inflicted by mechanized abuse and slaughter is caused by our desire for flavor at the expense of the animals we kill for food. Substituting plants, while respecting all creatures' will to live, is a positive action that moves society towards well-being and a peaceful life for all beings.

**"As medicines cure illness I take only what I need"**
One Buddhist perspective suggests that, ultimately, all food is medicine, and that the purpose of eating is merely to prevent the disease of hunger. If we don't eat, we starve and die, so food keeps us alive. Chefs and gourmet eaters might object that this view eliminates the joys of good eating and perhaps so. Nonetheless, contemplating food as medicine cuts through the desire for pleasurable flavors that rationalizes cruelty to animals. This contemplation reduces eating to fuel for the vehicle of the body, so that we can continue to live. This way, we eat to live, not live to

eat. Like contemplating our choices at the gas pump, cars meant to burn regular grade gas do not fare well burning high octane, diesel or kerosene. Humans, likewise, thrive on simpler, plant-based diets.

While bowing through Santa Barbara county, we met a high school biology teacher who approached us at lunch with a book in his hand. He introduced himself and said, "Look all around you at the plants under your feet. When offerings are scarce, if you can recognize just a few of the native plants along the California coastline, you can support yourselves and thrive."

He then handed us a copy of *Stalking the Wild Asparagus*, by the late Euell Gibbons, renowned naturalist and advocate of foraging edible native plants. The biology teacher warned us against picking mushrooms. He said, "There are old mushroom hunters and there are bold mushroom hunters, but there are no old and bold mushroom hunters. If you pick and eat mushrooms you can't clearly identify, you can die young!"

He taught us to distinguish hemlock (inedible and toxic) from its look-alike, Queen Anne's Lace (edible and useful.) After that encounter, we supplemented our diet with pot herbs such as sorrel, miner's lettuce, dandelions, and spices and medicinal herbs like fennel and yerba buena, rose hips, sage and peppermint. The connection between food and medicine became clearer with each bite of wild food. The green coastal fields turned into a living produce department before our eyes. Our gratitude to the planet for sustaining our lives and our health grew with each meal.

If hunger is an illness, then food is medicine. Once we recover from an illness we don't continue to take medicine; once our hunger is allayed we needn't continue to consume. The Middle Way, the method that leaves behind both excess and deficiency, can sustain our lives and that of the planet.

**"…To sustain my cultivation and to realize the Way;"**
This contemplation exhorts us to follow the Buddha's Way and the Bodhisattva's Way, paths of selfless spiritual practice on be-

half of others. The vision that powers this heroic dedication is the vision of connection among all beings, known to Buddhists as "same body, great compassion." It arises from the recognition that earth, water, fire and air, the four elements that comprise bodies, are shared in common with all living creatures past, present and future. Seeing this identity in our fundamental make-up can lead to the next awareness: that the inner spirit, or soul, or nature that inhabits our elemental bodies is likewise one, not two. This mealtime contemplation invites us to celebrate the awakened nature, identical in all beings.

Bowing along the San Mateo County coastline, to my delight, I read this sign posted at the gate to the Pigeon Point Lighthouse Station, near Pescadero, fifty miles south of San Francisco.

"No killing, hunting, fishing, trapping, harming or disturbing of wildlife in any way."
– By order of the commandant, U.S. Coast Guard, Pigeon Point Lighthouse Station

The sign brought tears of gratitude, imagining that the men and women in Coast Guard uniforms were using their military authority to defend the lives of animals, birds and sea creatures as well as protecting human interests along the coast. Perhaps this was an unusually compassionate commandant, or maybe compassion towards other species was an explicit policy for the Coast Guard. In any case it gave me goose bumps as I contemplated working alongside the US military to protect lives and save the environment for all beings. I salute the wise and compassionate Coast Guard commandant who embodied the vision of oneness and made the notion that we are interdependent and connected Pigeon Point Lighthouse's policy.

**"So we contemplate with gratitude on this offering today."**
Agronomists' studies show us that when our food is based on plants, instead of animal flesh, dairy, and eggs, the planet can

produce sufficient food to feed all humans and animals and put an end to starvation. The Five Contemplations in the Buddhist mealtime blessing bring that study to bear on my thoughts. The end to human starvation and cruelty to other species begins in my next thought.

How important is the wisdom of being content with our blessings? How important is it to not waste and instead to cherish and feel gratitude for the food on our table each day?

With every bite of food, The Five Contemplations connect body and spirit to the universe. My physical body's flesh, blood and breath are a microcosm of the planet Earth and its natural environment of continents, oceans, forests, mountains and atmosphere. This is the macrocosm where my physical and mental habits make their mark.

Employing the Five Contemplations in silence while eating has the potential to clarify our deeper connection to the entire web of life and to the fabric of production, consumption and transformation of energy that nourishes and sustains our lives. It generates a graceful inspiration to responsibility for the whole, and stewardship for the well-being of all.

# Compassion: The Heart of the Buddhist Teachings

TRACEY GLOVER

To be a Buddha means to be awake. Glimpsing the truth about the myriad ways we exploit and harm non-human animals, and recognizing our connection with them, is, for some of us, our first real moment of awakening. It was for the Buddha as well. It's said that the Buddha's first moment of awakening happened before he was known as the Buddha but still as the young Indian Prince Siddhartha. He was about seven years old when his family took him to a ploughing festival, which the king, his father, organized to celebrate the farming culture and the people who fed the kingdom. During the festival, the young prince watched the men drive the oxen who plowed the soil.

While the people celebrated, and were happy, the prince saw how hard the animals toiled and how much they suffered. He also saw all the other small animals, the mice, crickets, worms, and insects being displaced from their homes, and some even cut up by the blades of the plows. In that moment, he felt their suffering as if it were his own and felt a great compassion arising within his heart for them all. This is said to have been one of the most important moments in the Buddha's life, and that he spent the rest of his life trying to find and then teach a path that could lead to the end of suffering. It is clear to me that every vegan has the heart of an awakening Buddha and that no matter where we are on the path to an awakened life, a Buddhist practice can help us cultivate compassion and wisdom in order to be of maximum benefit to all sentient beings, while also enjoying the miracle of being alive.

As a child, I grew up in a home that was like a menagerie and always considered myself an animal lover. We had many cherished dogs and cats, as well as snakes, mice, fishes, rabbits, hamsters, and for a while a skunk (obviously, a terrible idea). We also ate animals without seeing any moral inconsistency. When I was about fifteen, during the late 1980s, I received a PETA mailer, and shortly thereafter read Peter Singer's *Animal Liberation*. Thanks to PETA and Singer, I learned for the first time what the animals in our modern agricultural system endure, and like the Buddha, and like all ethical vegans, I felt their suffering as if it were my own. I made the decision to go vegan.

Unfortunately, my first attempt at veganism was something of a failure. Living on a teenager's diet of potato chips, French fries, Oreos, fast food, and other convenience foods left me feeling unhealthy, and when everyone in my world at the time including parents, doctors, and friends all told me that my general lack of vibrant health was due to my strict vegan diet,

I believed them. I added eggs and dairy back into my diet but maintained an otherwise vegetarian diet for a few more years until, in my naiveté and ignorance, I somehow managed to convince myself that the government must have fixed all the problems that the PETA mailer and Singer's book had pointed out.

I distinctly remember how firm my faith was that the U.S. government was a benevolent and paternalistic entity whose purpose was to eliminate injustice and ensure fairness, decency, and the well-being of all members of our society, including the non-human animals. And though it would be downright laughable if it weren't so tragic, in my trusting, seventeen-year-old mind, I reasoned that if I knew about the horrible abuse of animals taking place throughout our food system, then surely the government must have known about it too. And if they knew, the only logical result was for them to fix these problems, because the government had the power to do that, and there was absolutely no moral ambiguity about what was right and wrong.

For a combination of reasons that I hope can help me better understand the obstacles pre-vegans face, I spent the next fifteen years bouncing back and forth between eating animals and being vegetarian, all the while struggling with myself and the non-vegan world. I think what prevented me from fully embracing veganism was my underlying worldview that the world was good. I couldn't accept that suffering on the scale that exists within animal agriculture in particular was even possible. With time, I learned more about the dark side of humanity, through media, books and movies, and in my own personal life. I read about the Holocaust and watched coverage of the Rwandan and Serbian genocides as they happened. But still, I couldn't let go of the Pollyannaish belief that we as a culture had evolved to be better, and that such atrocities were no longer possible here. Humans in other places apparently still did terrible things, I thought, and at one time in our history, we too had committed unconscionable crimes against humanity including massacring native Indians and enslaving African people, but surely we had learned our lesson and were no longer capable of such society-wide acts of violence or oppression.

I believed that while there would always be individual moral outliers in society, we as a society would not tolerate massive systematic torture of billions of sentient beings. The vegan agenda must be based on misinformation. I could not conceive that we would steal baby cows from their mothers, and then kill most of those fragile, terrified individuals in order for humans to drink the milk nature clearly intended for those babies. I was sure the labels on the dairy products that said "humane" must reflect humane treatment by any reasonable understanding of the word because, again, the government would ensure that.

My second vegan awakening finally came one day in the winter of 2005. My dog Penelope, whom I'd rescued from the local Humane Society, had been diagnosed with a large cancerous tumor behind her left eye. I'd opted to put her through radiation to save her life. By about three weeks into the treatment, she had a third degree burn caused by the radiation that covered the left side of her face. She was on pain medication, but was still obviously in pain, and the Elizabethan cone she had to wear to prevent her from bothering her open wound only amplified her discomfort. I felt like a horrible guardian/parent, and I regretted my decision to put her through this agony.

In the midst of this difficult time, I was getting more involved with a local anti-fur group and happened to watch an undercover film about the Chinese fur farm industry. The video included graphic, devastating footage of raccoon dogs being skinned alive, with one precious soul, whom I will never forget, blinking directly into the camera as she lay, skinned and discarded, on a pile of dead animals.

After watching the video, I remember crying for hours, sobbing and screaming into a pillow. I curled up in a little ball and covered my head trying to block out the world, filled with a sorrow that felt powerful enough to make the earth implode, but also filled with so much love for that one raccoon dog, and for my dear Penelope, and for every other animal in the world that suffered. In that moment, the truth of everything I'd been reading and denying for the preceding fifteen years hit me at once and cracked through the bubble of denial in which I'd been hiding. I knew we really did steal and kill all those babies, the humane labels were lies, and all the other horrors of animal agriculture were all true. The suffering was real, and I could never willingly or knowingly contribute to the suffering of another animal again. And so, for the second and final time, I went vegan, for life.

In the moment I made that commitment, I felt freed from the hard work of denial, and from all the wrestling I'd done with reality and with my own heart as I had struggled all those years to reconcile my love for animals with my choice to eat them and wear them. I felt that I was finally embracing my heart and choosing to live in alignment with my true nature.

I no longer had to struggle with myself, but that's when my struggle with society began. I realized that our whole culture is structured around an idea of human superiority, and built upon the mass exploitation, oppression, abuse, and killing of billions of sentient beings. I think almost all vegans I know have gone through at least a period (which tragically many never move through) of deep depression and rage caused by seeing the world through our new perception, aware of the cruelty and the suffering caused by humans. Many of us don't know what else to do but scream and yell, and attempt to force our friends, families, and everyone we meet to see what we see so that they will stop contributing to and causing this terrible suffering. But in doing so we're similar to that person who screams at someone who speaks a foreign language, mistakenly thinking that the louder we yell, the better we'll be understood.

For the first couple of years that I was vegan, I was filled with an anger at humanity bordering on hatred. I was depressed and frustrated with my own incapacity to help those in need. I was largely consumed with resentment and crushing sorrow and never seemed to know what to say to people to help make them understand so they would change their habits and stop hurting animals. I attended protests where angry and often intimidating activists yelled slurs at passersby through bullhorns. I watched graphic videos, because as painful as they were to watch, I knew the pain the animals endured was far greater. How could I look away when they suffered so much? I spent many nights lying wide awake with images of bloody slaughterhouses, and sad, frightened, injured animals floating through my mind.

After I'd been vegan a few years, a friend asked me to go to a yoga class while we were away at the beach for the weekend, and I agreed without realizing what I was in for. I'd taken many yoga classes at the gym in the past, but they had all been exclusively focused on the physical practice. This class was different. During the whole class, the instructor pushed us to find physical strength by looking inward and finding our strength within. He talked about ethics and pushed us hard, and I could feel my ego cracking as my knees wobbled and my muscles shook. At the end of class, he led us in a guided meditation that was intended to help us connect with the infinite peace, love, and light that he promised we all had at our core. But as we closed our eyes and plugged our ears and buzzed like bees (a form of meditation or pranayama called *bhramari*), I did not connect with peace, love, or light but with darkness and demons, with fear and pain, and I ended up leaving class in tears and sobbing for another two days afterwards. That's when I realized how much I needed that yoga class, how much suffering I was holding inside, and how much healing I had to do.

As a child of an atheist dad who'd been raised a Christian and an agnostic mom who'd grown up in an orthodox Jewish home, I was marginally exposed to the Judeo-Christian tradition growing up, but neither the Presbyterian church my dad took me to, nor the reform Jewish temple my mom made me attend ever resonated with me, or even my parents for that matter, in any spiritual way. We stopped attending before I turned ten. By the time I got to college, I basically thought spirituality and religion were for superstitious people, and because all of the spiritual traditions or teachers I'd ever known condoned eating animals, their claims at godliness and compassion rang hollow for me.

After my cathartic yoga experience, though, I felt some spiritual yearning stirring, a hunger for something I didn't yet know. I picked up some books on the philosophy of yoga and Buddhism. The teachings felt like they contained truth. Both of these related systems of spirituality seemed to revere the whole of life in a way that made sense to me. The teachings felt somehow familiar, like I was reading a truth that I'd always felt within but had never seen or heard before. They helped clarify what my heart had always sensed was true. Both Buddhism and yoga recognize the value of all life, are based upon a desire to do no harm to any sentient being, and moreover, to live with active, engaged compassion for all beings. Both see the unity and interconnection of all life, and teach that happiness comes from living in harmony with these insights into the nature of reality.

It was a revelation to realize that vegans aren't the moral extremists that many in our society would make us out to be, but we are in fact a living continuation of a tradition of non-harm and compassion that goes back thousands of years. The more I learned about the yogic and Buddhist teachings, the more I felt I'd found a whole set of spiritual traditions that deeply resonated with my heart, with my vegan philosophy and my way of life. I especially connected with the Buddhist Plum Village tradition, led by Thich Nhat Hanh, the Zen master and peace activist, who, in 2007, instructed all of the fifty plus monasteries who practice with him as their spiritual head to transition from being vegetarian (as they've always been) to becoming vegan for the benefit of sentient beings and the environment (though for the sake of full disclosure, I should note that the monasteries I've visited are more like ninety percent vegan).

In the *Yoga Sutras of Patanjali*, generally considered to be the foundation of classical yoga philosophy, we are given an eight-limbed system to achieve peace, happiness, wisdom, and ultimately union with the Divine both within ourselves and in everything else. The first limb comprises the moral injunctions, and the first of these is *ahimsa*, or non-harm to any sentient being. This is the heart and backbone of yoga practice and provides the foundation for ethical vegetarianism and especially in the modern world, ethical veganism. Similarly, while there are various Buddhist traditions that interpret the teachings somewhat differently, all Buddhists accept certain doctrines, including the Noble Eightfold Path and the Five Precepts. The First Precept is the injunction against taking any life, human or non-human. While some Buddhists, especially those following the Theravada tradition, believe the Buddha permitted his monks to eat meat if it was offered to them and not specifically killed for them, most Buddhist monks in the Mahayana tradition follow a vegan or at least a vegetarian diet. If we read the Buddha's teachings as a whole, it is clear that the injunction on taking life applies to what (or whom) we eat, given the emphasis on compassion for all sentient beings that pervades the entirety of Buddhist thought.

One of my favorite Buddhist stories tells about the enlightenment of the monk Asanga. Seeking enlightenment, Asanga went into the mountains and found a cave suitable for meditation. The story goes that after spending twelve years in meditation trying to see the Buddha, Asanga grew frustrated, gave up his search, and went down the mountain, but when he arrived in the town at the base of the mountain, he saw a woman cutting through a rock with a thin piece of thread. With great patience, she was able to wear down the rock with this thin thread. Asanga was inspired and thought, "If this woman can wear down a hard rock with a little piece of thread, how can I give up on my

very important aspiration to see the Buddha?" He went back up
the mountain and returned to his cave, where he spent another
twelve years in meditation. But still, he did not see the Buddha.
So again, he became frustrated, gave up his quest, and went back
down the mountain. This time on his way down he saw a large
boulder that had a hole in it and saw a tiny stream of water coming down the mountain, which, drop by drop over a long period
of time, had worn away this hole in the great boulder. And again,
Asanga thought, "How can I give up so easily? This little drop of
water makes a hole in this great boulder over time. In time, with
patience, I know I will see the Buddha." So again, he climbed
the mountain and returned to his cave. Another twelve years in
meditation passed, and still he did not see the Buddha.

For the last time, he decided he was really done for good
and went back down the mountain and back to the town. When
he got there, he saw a starving, mangy dog lying in the street, near
death he was so weak. No one would touch the dog because he
appeared diseased and dying. Asanga went to the dog to give him
comfort and offer him something to drink, but as he approached,
he saw the dog had a large gaping wound on his side that was
filled with maggots. He wanted to remove the maggots to alleviate
the dog's suffering, but he didn't even want to harm the maggots
because they too were sentient beings, so he bent down, and as
he gently stroked the dog, he stuck out his tongue in order to
allow the maggots to crawl onto it, and in that moment, the dog
disappeared, and in his place the Buddha Maitreya (the coming
Buddha) appeared before him. Asanga jumped up and bowed and
said "Lord Buddha, I have been meditating for so many years
to see you. Why do you appear now?" The Buddha smiled and
replied, "I was there with you all along, but it wasn't until you
opened your heart in deep compassion that you could see me."

Again, we see in the Buddhist tradition how vital a role
compassion plays in our path towards awakening. If we have
compassion in our hearts and we are in touch with that compas-

sion, we are already on the path towards enlightenment, and we cannot do anything intentionally to unnecessarily harm another living being. When our compassion is alive, the Buddha within us is present. This is why before every meal at the Plum Village monasteries, we contemplate our food with the prayer that "we keep our compassion alive by eating in such a way that reduces the suffering of living beings, stops contributing to climate change, and heals and preserves our precious planet."

I was drawn to Buddhism and yoga, and felt I'd found a safe space within these traditions, because of their emphasis on non-harm and compassion for all sentient beings. But more than just reinforcing the compassion I had already discovered within myself, they've helped me develop more understanding for humans, and they've helped me cope with the suffering of the world in a way that I believe helps me be a more effective activist, a force of light rather than darkness. As the Buddha says in the *Dhammapada*, "In this world, hate never yet dispelled hate. Only love dispels hate."

It seems to me entirely natural that in the face of abuse of innocent beings, we instinctively feel anger. When we see what's happening behind the closed doors and boarded up windows hiding the chickens, pigs, cows and other animals we use for food, or the fur-bearing animals we kill for their beautiful coats, or the animals we exploit for entertainment, and when we see into the laboratories where monkeys, mice, and other animals are being tortured, or the beautiful wild animals both large and small who are being hunted for sport or for food, it seems a perfectly reasonable response to be enraged or devastated, or to become depressed. I know that when I witness any form of cruelty or suffering, especially the kind that is routinely captured in undercover videos, I can become so overwhelmed with anger and sadness that I have often felt I simply could not bear this world anymore. The word compassion means to "suffer with." But as Thich Nhat Hanh says, we cannot drown in our own suffering. We cannot offer happiness if we don't have it within ourselves. Many animal activists seem to think that we need to suffer because the animals suffer. And of course we do suffer with them, but we also need to learn to cultivate enough peace and love within ourselves that we can help heal the world.

There is a story the Buddha once told to his monks about the capacity of our hearts. He said, "If you have a handful of salt and you throw it in a glass of water, can you drink the water?" And the monks responded "No, of course not. It would be too salty." "But," the Buddha said, "if you take that handful of salt and you throw it into a big river, then could you drink that water?" And the monks reply "Yes, of course because the river is so big and flowing, and it can dissolve that little bit of salt." So too, the Buddha says we must have hearts like a great river, and cultivate so much compassion, joy, and equanimity within ourselves that we can dissolve the salts of fear and delusion, and in that way be a source of liberation and happiness to others.

About two months after the Buddha's enlightenment, he delivered his first discourse to the five monks who formed his original forest dwelling *sangha*, or spiritual community. In this first discourse, he established some of the most important and defining teachings thereafter associated with Buddhism. He taught the importance of avoiding two extremes. On one hand, he taught, we can be caught-up in worldly pleasures and pursuits, driven by personal desire, decadence, and the never-ending search for pleasure, which is based in ignorance of the true nature of reality, and which ultimately and inevitably leads to unhappiness. On the other hand, we can also be caught by the other extreme of self-deprivation, mortification, and self-sacrifice to the degree that we have no joy or happiness and are still doomed to suffer, and make others around us suffer too. The Buddha taught that there was a middle path that was preferable to these extremes, one that could free us from personal suffering, and help us lead others out of suffering as well.

I look back on my pre-vegan years as largely being characterized by the first extreme, seeking pleasure and personal happiness, ignorant about the effects my actions had on other beings, and despite seeking personal happiness, never really attaining it in any lasting or meaningful way. I also now see that during the first few years of my life as a vegan, I bordered on the second extreme, self-flagellating by watching all those videos and thinking about the animals' suffering all the time, as if I needed to suffer constantly to help them.

Gradually, as I began to deepen my yoga and meditation practices, I began to find that middle path. I'm still making adjustments, but I've learned that I can do much more for the animals by finding balance and happiness in my own life. Once we become aware of the effects our actions have on others, we no longer derive happiness from activities that harm others. Our happiness is no longer selfish or harmful. Rather, it is found in being kind, in opening our hearts, in making meaningful, loving connections with others and the natural world, and appreciating and supporting the beauty and joy in the world. I still feel the pain of the world, but I also see the beauty of it and understand that I don't have to be unhappy to help others.

When we are consumed by the energy of anger, or stuck in judgmental thinking, we drive people away. We also lose our own peace. When I sit in quietness, and breathe into my heart, whether I'm on my meditation cushion, or on my back porch with a cat on my lap, or even walking through the meat section at the grocery store, what I find is love, a deep love not dependent on circumstances. That is the energy that heals from within, and that will heal our world. It attracts people to our way of life rather than pushing them away.

As activists, our job is to help awaken the compassion that exists in the hearts of others. I've learned that I'm more comfortable advocating from a place of compassion than a place of judgment or anger, in large part because people respond so much better to me when I'm kind, friendly, and understanding. I believe we are more effective advocates when we are rooted in the compassion that lies at the heart of every vegan, every Buddha, and all of us, rather than the anger and despair that come from the inability to alleviate suffering.

When we engage in debates with others from a place of anger or judgment, we immediately put our interlocutor on the defensive. Both of our egos take over like a tarp covering the ground, preventing the rain from watering the soil. I believe there is a Buddha-to-be in the heart of us all. Few vegans were born vegan. Most of us grew up eating animal products, but there was always a vegan-to-be within us. The more we can see this potential in others, the more easily we can help water the seeds of compassion within them, like the great Bodhisattva *Sadaparibhuta*, who says to all he meets, "You are someone of great value, you have Buddha nature; I see this potential in you." When we see the positive potential in others, we give them inspiration, support, and confidence to be the best version of themselves.

The Buddha's journey to full enlightenment began when he saw the plight of non-human animals. When he empathized with them, his heart naturally opened to them. Vegan living is based on this insight into the importance of caring concern for animals, and it can put us on a path towards enlightenment. I believe we all have a vegan heart, and that we have the heart of a Buddha and the capacity to be awake and to see clearly. In seeing clearly, we can recognize our connection with all others and the whole of nature. The path of the Buddha is one of opening and of being present for those who suffer, instead of turning away. Above all, it is one of cultivating the seed of compassion within us until it is without limit or boundary. This is the energy that can heal the world. As the Buddha taught:

> Just as a mother with her own life
> Protects her child, her only child, from harm,

So within yourself let grow
A boundless love for all creatures.
Let your love flow outward through the universe,
To its height, its depth, its broad extent,
A limitless love, without hatred or enmity.
Then, as you stand or walk,
Sit or lie down,
As long as you are awake,
Strive for this with a one-pointed mind;
Your life will bring heaven to earth.
-from the *Metta Sutta*

# Descending into the Canyon: A Heart Broken Open

JOANNE CACCIATORE

*The first peace, which is the most important, is that which comes within the souls of people when they realize their relationship, their oneness with the universe and all its powers, and when they realize that at the center of the universe dwells the Great Spirit, and that this center is really everywhere, it is within each of us.*

—Black Elk, Oglala Sioux

When I was seven years old, I announced to my family that I was done eating animals. It was 1972, and that was a revolutionary statement for a little Sicilian girl. I've always had a heart for animals. I have rehomed countless spiders and beetles, and nursed bunnies and birds back to health. While I don't completely understand what animal suffering stirs in me, somehow, in the marrow of my bones, I have always felt a sense of connection to animals.

More than that, I've had a nagging sense of personal duty to show compassion to animals, and I've been deeply pained by the cruelty inflicted on them by humans. From circuses to food production, from farming to films, the exploitation of animals has felt morally repugnant to me from an early age. These feelings have been central to my identity and I've been determined to live my life in alignment with them.

I raised my children according to these values and learned how to explain to others why I wouldn't participate in activities that exploited animals or eat foods derived by abusing animals. The philosophical underpinnings of my life have reflected the core reverence I feel for all forms of life. Remaining sensitive to the natural world has been essential.

But the natural world can be destructive and with forces like hurricanes, floods, droughts, fires, and earthquakes, death may come. I have five children. When my fourth child, Cheyenne, died suddenly and unexpectedly during her birth, I descended into a shattering grief that stole my will to live and erased meaning from my life. I couldn't eat, sleep, or function. The grief, fear, and despair of her death, and the way others turned away from my intense suffering, exacerbated my loneliness, and took a severe toll on my mother-heart.

I did not recover from this trauma, but rather gained a capacity to help support others through the natural, not pathological, spiritual crucible of grief. Today, I am a professor at Arizona State University with a research focus on traumatic grief and am creator of a foundation that serves individuals and families suffering with the death of their child. My goal is to help free others from feeling as alone as I'd felt in 1994.

During these years I gradually discovered Buddhism. In Zen Buddhism, I found a philosophy, an array of practices, and a way of being that fits me well and has helped deepen my commitment to *ahimsa*, nonharmfulness to all sentient beings and the Earth. Everything in the Zen teachings encourages full engagement with life. The philosophy, taught through Zen meditation and the existential *koan* practices, rather than being confined to conceptual metaphysics, illuminates the complex dynamics of lived experience and helps cultivate strength and wisdom to achieve compassionate unity in diversity. The mind of meditation becomes the body-mind of living. I practice sitting and walking meditation, as well as a barefoot desert hiking practice like the Carmelite monks of the 16th century.

The gifts of Zen also include more flexibility in shifting identities. I can choose and take positions while appreciating context and limits, and while also releasing into emptiness. For me, what's been especially important is how Zen allows me to appreciate the precious particularity of each individual in the world as well as the interconnectedness of these individual lives. This understanding has continued to grow, not only from the study and practice of Zen, but also from walking the path of a vegan life.

In April of 2015, I was pressed to deepen my understanding of both Zen and veganism, and to go beyond ahimsa as passive nonharmfulness into action propelled by the spirit of the Buddhist teachings. It was a chilly spring morning when I began my hike to Havasupai Falls, a remote location deep in the heart of the Grand Canyon that I'd always wanted to visit. In stark contrast to the barren topography of Hualapai Hilltop where hikers begin the long descent into the canyon, the lush and tropical falls at the bottom of the canyon boast nearly 2,000 species of vascular plants, more than 60 varieties of moss, and

200 species of lichen. After months of preparation for the 13-mile descent, I began my trek, with my camping gear on my back, not knowing how my life would change that day. I would never get beyond the first three minutes of that hike.

On this particular trail, people often use mules and horses to help carry their packs, coolers, and even lawn chairs. I felt a nagging concern for the animals, verbalizing that to an accompanying friend. Then, just as we turned the first corner starting down the steep, barren trail, I witnessed a scene that still remains etched in my mind and my heart. A horse carrying backpacks, tents, and other supplies that were tied to a wooden frame mounted to his back had fallen to the ground. A young native man was kicking and punching him, trying to force him back up on his feet. I was stunned. I screamed at the man to stop. He stopped but looked squarely and threateningly into my eyes. My heart was pounding loudly against my chest and I started to cry.

I imagine it was my tears, well-practiced after 21 years of crying for my deceased child, that disturbed him, as he swiftly took his other horses around to the top of the trail, leaving the wounded one on the ground near me. I bent down and gently touched him. He flinched. I wept more, apologizing to him for the brutality he was enduring at the hands of a human.

We stayed with this horse as he lay helplessly on the ground. He was bleeding from his head and legs. This once majestic creature, now limp and terrified, was in immeasurable suffering. I was crying, openly, as others hiked passed us, some asking if I was okay. I exclaimed, "This horse, this horse is hurt! He's been abused!" But there was no cell service or police because of our remote location. The other hikers all walked by quickly. Only one stopped to offer her water bottle for the horse.

The horse was laboring to breathe. We removed the heavy packs, the saddle and the wooden frame used to tie the packs from his weary, sweat-drenched back. This revealed open and bleeding wounds. His knees and legs were bleeding, he had lacerations on his belly, and he was severely emaciated and dehydrated. Vertebrae were protruding through his skin. His hair and skin were worn down, exposing both hipbones. I stood up and my head spun in circles. It was one of the most terrible things I have ever seen, save the limp body of my dead daughter that I held two decades earlier (which came up in my memory strongly in that moment).

Then the horse and I looked into each other's eyes, and he allowed me to stroke him. Something ineffable overcame me: I was that horse many years ago. *I*, too, had suffered as he was suffering and knew his fear and despair. I, too, had once given up and lost my will to live. Now, as I stroked this horse, for the first time in my life, I had a direct and powerful experience of oneness. I was that horse and that horse was me.

I promised him that I would help him, though I didn't understand how or why. I felt that somehow my daughter, Cheyenne, was involved in this as well.

We sat with him for about an hour as he rested on the ground, and as people passed by, looking up and looking down, but few looking at the horror of the scene. I searched the trail, gathering a few strands of scarce grass to offer him. I held his head and he rested in my lap. I could not leave him. This precious life, my brother horse, child of Earth, just like me, just like us all.

I repeatedly told him how sorry I was that humans did this to him. Our suffering merged into one suffering. I vowed: "Please remember me. I'm going to get you out of here. I'm going to help you, I promise..."

We offered to buy him from his owner, twice. Vociferously, the abusive owner declined. And just like that, with pieces of my heart shattered on the parched trailhead, our plans abruptly ended. I left without the horse that day, feeling like I'd left a piece of myself, as if I'd given up on myself. And as much pain and sorrow as I felt, I allowed those deep feelings and I stayed with them, right in the center of my core, until they transformed into what I can only call fierce compassion.

Within minutes after we got back to the car, I felt a wellspring of wild and untamed fury in my belly. I was going to do everything and anything to save him.

It was nearly two hours before I could get cell service to make calls. And I made many calls. I called the forest service, the sheriff, the FBI, local police, animal control, legislators, congressional leaders, horse rescues, animal protection groups, superintendents, police chiefs, lawyers, an animal activist colleague, friends, neighbors, strangers, this specific community's police, and their governmental leaders. For two days, I stayed in my pajamas, made nearly one hundred phone calls and sent more than one hundred emails. I felt hopeless, and even though so many others explicitly told me that the situation was hopeless, I *had* to keep trying. This animal's life mattered. I had to exhaust every possible means to rescue him and get him the medical care he so desperately needed. I was told that there was "nothing anyone can do." Repeatedly.

But, I was not going to stop. I couldn't. I saw into this animal's soul, and I loved him.

Then, a holy moment.

One person heard my plea and a team of governmental leaders got behind my effort.

Seven more phone calls, six emails, and three days later, I got the call.

"Dr. Cacciatore," he said, "how soon can you get here?"

"What?" I asked. "What, really, really? Seriously?"

"Yes ma'am..."

That call came in around four in the afternoon and by ten that night we had a trailer. At two in the morning, two heroic men made the five-hour drive and then descended by foot many miles to rescue and rehome this horse. I held fast hope throughout the night and waited, thinking he would likely die.

I wanted him to survive long enough to know what it felt to be loved and safe.

And so, I waited.

Sixteen hours later, the horse, still alive, stepped off the trailer, tentative, emaciated, dehydrated, and frightened. He stumbled off the trailer, let out a feeble whinny, and walked straight over to me as if to thank me for keeping my promise. To say this was an emotional reunion would be woefully understated.

I named him Chemakoh, a Pima word meaning *"two souls who came together as one in destiny."*

All my life, I had wanted to hike to Havasupai Falls. I had waited for the right time, and as fate would have it, I was never able to start the hike at all. Now I understand why my heart longed to go there. I was in that place to meet and rescue Chemakoh; all these years for just this one moment in time.

The first few days after he arrived home were tenuous. We didn't know if he'd survive. His wounds were deep, and bones had eroded through the hair and flesh on his spine and hips. There were holes worn through to muscle on both sides of his girth. Some wounds were obviously infected, while others scarred over from years of wounding. We faced a long road toward his rehabilitation, both physical and psychological.

Chemakoh is still with us, the most gentlemanly stallion most have ever met. Three years later, he loves even though he didn't know love. He is genial despite the cruelty foisted on him. He connects despite years of fear and loneliness. He's also a terrific teacher for the grieving families with whom I work, along with seventeen other rescued animals now at Selah Carefarm, a sanctuary we created as a place of respite for wounded animals and grieving families to come together in the mutuality of both suffering and compassion.

The only way to real peace in the world is through making an effort to understand that suffering connects us all in oneness. Being awake means that when we can, we should act with fierce compassion to save the life of another and to promote non-violence for all living beings. Chemakoh knew grief and fear, despair and loneliness. He knew how it felt when people averted their gaze, unwilling to see the pain of the other. They walked past him, passively enabling his continued abuse.

I, too, knew these horrors intimately. I felt the same grief, fear, despair and loneliness. Others turned away from my grief-stricken mother's heart. I, too, was hopeless, on death's door, uncertain of my will or ability to live. Our suffering was the same suffering. My encounter with Chemakoh affirmed that violence against animals anywhere is violence against our very humanity everywhere. Compassion toward animals is also compassion in support of our humanity. We can, and we should, do better for all beings, everywhere. This is the truth of oneness. Nothing less.

For me, my active veganism, my willingness to gently educate others and influence by example, as well as my commitment to fierce compassion in helping other beings in need, is well expressed in the Four Bodhisattva Vows:

> Creations are numberless, I vow to free them.
> Delusions are inexhaustible, I vow to transform them.
> Reality is boundless, I vow to perceive it.
> The Enlightened Way is unsurpassable, I vow to embody it.

# Awakening of the Heart

SHERRY MORGADO

I think I can confidently say that both my vegan and Buddhist awakenings had their birth in the same event I witnessed as a child. Over these many years of my life since this event, it has become clearer to me that to practice and take refuge in the Dharma means to make an effort to express our compassion and wisdom through the practice of veganism as well.

I grew up on a small farm in central California, the granddaughter and daughter of Portuguese immigrants. My family raised about five steers each year. As a child, I spent many happy hours in the pastures with those cows, enjoying their peaceful companionship as they munched happily on grass and hay, mooing and bellowing to each other. I loved to pet their smooth and silky hair, and laughed when they licked and suckled my fingers.

One day, when I was nine years old, I stayed home from school due to illness. It turned out to be a day, I realize now, that changed my life dramatically, because it significantly shifted my consciousness about suffering. It was the day that my father had arranged for the butcher to come to our property and slaughter one of our steers. Before this day, I did not understand where the meat that filled our large freezer came from. I suppose I knew it was from animals, but which animals? Afterward there was no doubt. I don't think my father realized that the sound of the large rumbling truck and the loud voices of men had caught my attention while I was lying down in my bedroom.

Curious, I went outside to see what the commotion was. Within a matter of minutes, I saw one of my sweet bovine friends, who had nuzzled me and given me companionship, shot in the head with a gun. What followed was the horror of seeing his body cinched and hoisted up via a crane on the back of the truck where they proceeded to cut his throat, skin his body and cut him into pieces right in front of my eyes— pieces that were later wrapped in white paper and stored in our freezer. Those pieces my mother would then cook and serve us each night. A gut-wrenching realization washed over me: every night I was eating the body of a sweet, gentle creature who had loved his life, just as I did. I knew from my hours spent with these cows that they felt love and fear, that they yearned for companionship, and that they had a purpose on this Earth, beyond the way that humans controlled and exploited their bodies and their lives.

How could my parents do this? What could possibly justify the murder I had just witnessed, the murder of someone we had loved and nurtured? Like the song "Meat is Murder" by The Smiths says, "a death for no reason is murder." At that moment I felt that I was drowning in suffering—the suffering of the cow through our family's betrayal, the suffering my parents were actively taking part in, the suffering I felt at being duped and misled. No one had ever told me at dinner that I was eating the body parts of the animals I knew and loved. Meat was one of those things we didn't talk about, unlike the vegetables that came from our garden, or the fruit we picked from a friend's tree, which we discussed to great extent. Meat was omnipresent, yet silent.

All I knew as a nine-year-old child was that I had just seen hell, and I knew, deep down, that none of this violence and suffering was necessary. And at that moment, I also realized that it wasn't just my beloved friend who had been killed for his flesh—it was hundreds of thousands of animals every single day (I now know that number is actually millions of animals per day). A strong vegetarian seed was planted in my consciousness that day. While I tried very hard to be a vegetarian at that tender age of nine, my family was not supportive or helpful and I struggled. But I knew when the conditions were favorable, that somehow, I would be a pure vegetarian and would work to advocate for animals.

At the age of eighteen, while browsing in my local community library one day, I came across the section on Buddhism, and picked up the book *Zen Mind, Beginner's Mind* by Shunryu Suzuki Roshi. This book presented radical ideas that resonated strongly with me in regards to reality, mind, and an alternative way of being. At that time, as a young adult, I felt weighed down by the cultural norms and expectations of the society of which I was part, and was certainly up for some rebellion, as many young adults are. Suzuki Roshi's statement, "When you study Buddhism, you should have a general housecleaning of your mind," was like a flash of lightening in the darkness. I knew my mind was travelling well-worn paths of conditioning and expectations.

Hearing there was another way to be in this world was like a cool breeze on a hot day.

Although it took a number of years after that for me to formally become a Buddhist by taking my refuge vows and receiving the precepts, I began a spiritual quest at that point, and the teachings of the Buddha were always at the center of my studies and contemplations. This was about the same time that I left home for college and signed up for the vegetarian meal plan at my dorm. Finally, meat was no longer on my plate. I assumed at that point that anyone practicing Buddhism was also a vegetarian or vegan—to me, it seemed a given that serene minds, compassionate hearts, and wise actions are all built on the foundation of a peaceful diet and reverence for all life. I believed that anyone sincerely walking a spiritual path would never intentionally and unnecessarily cause suffering to another living being.

However, I learned that the truth was a bit different, because I discovered Buddhist practitioners who didn't give a second thought about eating meat on a daily basis, much less questioning the suffering behind dairy products and eggs. How could this be? I think there is a tendency in our modern society to use Buddhist teachings and practices in an effort to simply "better our own life." Practitioners can focus on meditation as a way to calm their mind and relieve stress, rather than also using it as a way to generate compassion and wisdom. Teachings on the ultimate reality and on emptiness can be construed as an invitation to simply negate the world we live in and to dismiss concerns about suffering as the karmic outcome of previous lives.

But *samsara* (conditioned existence) is also real, and living beings suffer greatly. We have a wise and compassionate teacher to help us on the path of liberation for ourselves and for all with whom we share this Earth. We who have been fortunate to find the teachings of the Dharma in this lifetime are called to use those teachings to promote what the Buddha started nearly 2,600 years ago: a revolution of compassion and wisdom that makes this Earth a reflection of our true nature. We are called to be bold and authentic because we are endowed with the heart and mind of a Buddha.

When he came to the end of his life, the Buddha said that his teachings focused on helping people understand the causes of suffering and the path to end suffering, and nothing else. The Buddha was clearly moved by the suffering he saw in the world, both that experienced by humans as well as by the other creatures with whom we share the world. As a child, he was moved to tears by the death of the insects and worms he saw killed as the Earth was tilled in his village. As an adolescent, he came to the aid of a swan his cousin had shot, and fearlessly stood his ground in opposing his family regarding the innocence of the swan and the needless suffering that had been inflicted upon this bird.

Time and time again, through his actions, teachings, and directives to his monks, his message was clear: these teachings on suffering and the cessation of suffering apply to all sentient beings, not just humans. At the time of his enlightenment, he spoke of the Buddha-nature present in all beings, and repeated this throughout his lifetime. The Buddha saw clearly that suffering is generated in this world through unwholesome acts such as killing, stealing and exploiting, and that wisdom shows us the unity of life, and interconnections between each and every thing in the universe. When we harm one, we harm all, including ourselves. He gave us a clear roadmap to stop creating suffering through the practice of the precepts and the Noble Eightfold Path. He also asked us to look deeply within to touch our inherent Buddha-nature, and to live from this place of truth, and not from the conditioning of our family and society.

Though I didn't grow up in a vegetarian or vegan family, my life now as a Buddhist means that I live as a vegan, because compassion calls this to be the guiding force of my life as I practice the Dharma. Confining, commodifying, and killing animals to take and use their flesh, milk and eggs is nothing other than cruel, leading to immense terror and pain unnecessarily inflicted upon sentient beings who are my sisters and brothers in samsara. The abuse of these industries is well documented. We need only be willing to look at the realities involved and open ourselves to the consequences of these realities.

Being a Buddhist vegan provides me with a roadmap as I navigate the various paths and decisions of my life, helping me stay on a compassionate course, even when my self-interest would lead me elsewhere. I feel I've been given a rare gift: a human life in which I've encountered the Dharma and the opportunity to live in a place and time when plant-based foods are abundant and animals need not suffer for me to nourish this impermanent body. There is deep peace within me as I walk this Buddhist vegan path, an authentic peace that I nourish in such a way that the world can also be at peace. The Buddha is alive within all of us who practice his path; we bring his teachings to this modern world in our actions and our way of life. Our actions are, ultimately, all we have to stand on. We are called to ask ourselves if the Buddhist teachings have transformed us deeply so that we can transform this world of suffering.

As a nine year old, I felt profoundly the suffering caused by the killing of animals, although I had no real framework within which to begin to transform it. As an eighteen year old, I discovered that there was a path to a radical and loving way of being in the world. They joined forces in my consciousness and awakened my heart. While it took time for this consciousness to ripen and for my heart to open, when they did, a force of joy arose within me. When I took my refuge vows and received the precepts in the lineage of my teacher, the Zen master Thich Nhat Hanh, I was given the Dharma name "Joyful Awakening of the Heart." I cried when I received the name because it so well described my spiritual journey in which veganism and Buddhism are intertwined, or "inter-are," as my teacher would say. I invite all of my sisters and brothers in the Dharma to join this same joyful vegan journey. Together we can transform this world of suffering.

# Eat Your Way to Wisdom

MASTER XIANQING

~~~~~~~~~~~~~~~~~~~~~~~~~~~~~~~~~~~~~~~~~~~~~~~~~~~~~~~~~

The common purpose of all different religions and philosophies is to explore the truth of the world and the universe. The sages, with their own thinking and understanding, reveal the truth about the relationship between humans, the animal kingdom and the environment, as well as how to live in accordance with wisdom so as to experience authentic happiness and peace.

Abstaining from killing and being vegetarian are not principles that were initiated by Buddhism, nor are they unique to Buddhism. At around 1000 BC, the idea of advocating a vegetarian diet appeared in both India and the eastern Mediterranean. According to the historical records, Pythagoras, a Greek philosopher in the sixth century BC, was the earliest vegetarian in the Mediterranean area, who advocated replacing meat with vegetarian food, and asked his disciples to do the same. From the time of Plato onwards, many philosophers such as Plotinus, Epicurus and Plutarch, also advocated vegetarianism. They did this because they believed that the soul could be reincarnated.

The essential difference between Buddhism and other religions is that the Buddha perceived the truth of Egolessness (*anatta*). The advocacy of a vegetarian diet in Buddhism is a concrete manifestation of the spirit of no ego. In addition, it is also a form of practice through which Buddhists can cultivate compassion. In that it complies with the laws of nature, the vegetarian way of life advocated by Buddhism is not only instructive to Buddhists, but can also bring comfort and greater awareness to non-Buddhists.

Eating meat can temporarily satisfy a desire, but it breaches and damages the equal relationship between humankind and other sentient beings. Therefore, a long-term adherence to this unhealthy lifestyle can only bring harm to ourselves and others. The scientific community reveals the harm of being a meat-eater and the benefits of being vegetarian from a perspective that is focused on this life. (We use the word vegetarian to include abstention from dairy and eggs, which are products of the meat industry.) However, Buddhism explains from the perspective of infinite life that a vegetarian diet can not only benefit one in the next life, but can improve physical and mental health and increase wisdom in this life, even in the present moment. Furthermore, because of the proliferation of meat culture, our planet has been overwhelmed. Given this situation, vegetarianism plays an important role in alleviating the Earth's burden, preventing environmental degradation, and benefiting all sentient beings on the Earth.

Buddhism is broad and profound, not only providing us with the reasons and benefits of being vegetarian in the teachings, but also establishing related precepts to help practitioners slowly change from being omnivorous to practicing vegetarianism. What's more, in the history of Chinese Buddhism, many eminent monks' vegetarian habits and outstanding actions have set a good example for the public to persist in following vegetarianism, and build their confidence. Moreover, the vegetarian culture and traditions in Chinese Buddhist monasteries have a history of over two thousand years, which mandates that the Buddha's teachings on diet be fully practiced by monks and practitioners.

Compassion is the Buddha's original intention, and the fundamental purpose of promoting vegetarianism is based on compassion. Buddhism teaches that all sentient beings follow endlessly repeated cycles made up of the six-fold paths: heaven (*devagati*), the human world (*manussagati*), the asura realm (*asuratta*), hell (*narakagati*), the ghost realm (*petagati*) and the animal world (*tiracchanayonik*) due to different karma. As sentient beings upon the six-fold paths, animals are equal to humankind in that they have spirits and Buddha nature, and will ultimately attain Buddhahood. Killing sentient beings for food goes against the fundamental spirit of "never harming sentient beings" in Buddhism.

In the *Lankavatara Sutra*, the Buddha answers the question put forward by Mahamati in telling the crowd that eating meat will destroy the seeds of compassion, but abstaining from eating meat can quickly lead to the supreme wisdom of enlightenment.

Pray tell me, Bhagavan, Tathagata, Arhat, Fully-Enlightened One regarding the merit of not eating meat, and the vice of meat-eating; thereby I and other Bodhisattva-Mahasattvas of the present and future may teach the Dharma to make those beings abandon their greed for meat, who, under the influence of the habit-energy belonging to the carnivorous existence, strongly crave meat-food. These meat-eaters thus abandoning their desire for [its] taste will seek the Dharma for their food and enjoyment, and, regarding all beings with love as if they were an only child, will cherish great compassion towards them. Cherishing [great compassion], they will discipline themselves at the stages of Bodhisattvahood and will quickly be awakened in supreme enlightenment; or staying a while at the stage of Sravakahood and Pratyekabuddhahood, they will finally reach the highest stage of Tathagatahood.

In the *Surangama Sutra* that is highly respected by the Chan (Zen) tradition, the Buddha pointed out that those who eat meat, no matter how good they are at meditating, cannot overcome afflictions and escape from birth and rebirth.

You should know that these people who eat meat may gain some awareness and may seem to be in samadhi, but they are all great *rakshasas* (demons). When their retribution ends, they are bound to sink into the bitter sea of birth and death. They are not disciples of the Buddha. Such people as these kill and eat one another in a never-ending cycle. How can such people transcend the Triple Realm?

In the *Angulimaliya Sutra*, the Buddha pointed out that the reason why no Buddhas eat meat is that they have understood that self is other and other is self, "the meat of others is the meat of mine." The Buddha praised Mahakasyapa because he had a very high level of practice when it came to eating, and wherever he was and no matter what situation he encountered, he would always be calm and his heart and mind would never be moved.

In the places where he begged there were all sorts of people. Some said they had no food, and some scolded and insulted him, however, Mahakasyapa just replied with blessings and left calmly, with his heart unmoved. If some said they had food, Mahakasyapa refrained himself from greed, replied with blessings and left calmly, with his heart unmoved.

The Buddhist form of vegetarianism involves not only quitting all animal-sourced foods, but also the "Five Spices."

According to the *Brahmajala Sutra*, monks should refrain from the five acrid and strong-smelling vegetables: garlic, three kinds of onions, and leeks. Whoever eats them commits a slight but impure crime.

There are two reasons for abstaining from eating the five spices. Firstly, after eating garlic and scallions, the strong smell will affect others. According to the precepts, those who eat the five spices should live alone or stand a few paces away from others, as well as sit in the downwind position or repeatedly rinse the mouth to dissipate the smell, all of which aims to minimize disturbance of others' practice.

Secondly, eating the five spices disturbs practice. The *Surangama Sutra* reveals that those who want to practice meditation need to stop eating the five acrid and strong-smelling vegetables, because these vegetables will affect people's physical and mental state whether raw or cooked. Eating the raw vegetables will make people become irritable, while eating them cooked will bring people lust and impulsiveness.

When the Buddha gave the first Dharma talk, he pointed out that people could eat "triply clean meat" in exceptional circumstances, but before entering nirvana, the Buddha explained the cause and intention behind eating "triply clean meat." According to the *Nirvana Sutra*, a disciple asked the Buddha why the "triply clean meat" that was permitted in the first Dharma talk was forbidden now? The Buddha answered that religious discipline is like a flight of stairs that ascends step by step. At that time, there were some people who had suitable foundations and opportunities to convert to Buddhism, however, if required not to eat meat, their failure to keep to this stricture might give rise to obstacles in their practice. Therefore, out of great compassion, the Buddha allowed them to eat "triply clean meat" at first, and then gradually guided them to stop eating meat altogether. Due to historical and cultural reasons, strictly following a vegetarian diet became the most common situation for Chinese Buddhist monks and practitioners.

During the era when the Buddha was alive, monks and nuns fed themselves by going door to door asking for free food or were supported by householders. To make it easy for people to offer food, the Buddha did not, at this time, require that only vegetarian food should be eaten. When Buddhism was first introduced to China, the masters who accepted the emperor's patronage ate triply clean meat occasionally.

During the Northern and Southern Dynasties (420-589), the emperor Liangwu who believed firmly in Buddhism wrote four essays under the title, "Quit Meat and Wine," in order to oppose meat-eating and promote a vegetarian lifestyle, which led to the requirement of all monks and nuns to quit meat. Killing animals for sacrificial offerings was prohibited as well. At that time, almost half of the people followed a vegetarian lifestyle. Since then, it has become a rule that monks and nuns are required to be vegetarian. This rule has lasted down to the present day, so that Buddhist monks, nuns, and lay people are all vegetarian.

Chinese *Chan* (Zen) Buddhism believes in integrating practice into daily life by habitually doing small daily actions in the Chan way. From a monk or a nun's point of view, eating can be an opportunity to practice Chan. According to Master Lianchi: "the opportunity to practice Chan appears with every bite you take while eating, with every step you make while walking," which enables practitioners to take advantage of an opportunity to practice Chan and experience its miraculous effects in daily life.

The sixth Chan patriarch Hui Neng pointed out in *The Sixth Patriarch's Dharma Jewel Platform Sutra* that "Being separate from external marks is 'Chan.' Not being confused inwardly is 'concentration.'" To enter the state of meditation, one should stay away from greed and hatred which come from eating meat. Therefore, food is seen by monks and nuns as a medicine to cure the disease of hunger and to maintain the body itself.

In daily life, food ranks first amongst the causes of human greed. In Chinese monasteries, having meals is also a kind of practice that is called the Five Contemplations among which the third contemplation is to safeguard the mind against all error, and to not give rise to hatred or greed. Monks and nuns don't attach themselves to delicious food. Instead, they consider the process of how hard it was for the people who worked to produce all the food, no matter whether the food is simple or complex. In addition, they are not picky over the quality of the food. This is because not being greedy and not eating too much are of great benefit to our physical health and daily practice. Eating too much can give rise to a great many afflictions, such as doing harm to physical health and affecting practice.

Chinese Chan Buddhism believes that practice is inseparable from living and that every little thing in our life can be a form of practice, such as cooking, eating, and doing the dishes. If the cook prepares meals without kindness and compassion, the food will be bland and the people who eat it will certainly notice. In Buddhist monasteries, the monk who is in charge of cooking meals is called Dian Zuo. From ancient times down to the present day when a Dian Zuo is elected, only someone who is outstanding can obtain the position. This is because there is an old saying in Chinese Buddhism: "the monastery kitchen is the 'birth place' of Great Masters." This emphasizes the idea that practice and living, i.e. cooking, are inseparable.

The historical development of Chinese culinary culture has been influenced by Chinese Buddhist vegetarianism. During the Southern Song Dynasty (960-1271), vegetarian restaurants already existed in Bian Liang, the capital city of the Southern Dynasty, and the development of vegetarian style dishes continued apace during the Yuan Dynasty (1271-1368), Ming Dynasty (1368-1644) and Qing Dynasty (1644-1911).

There was an imperial kitchen in the royal palace during the Qing Dynasty. The people there created more than 200 vegetarian dishes during this period, and the cooking level reached such a high level that vegetarian dishes became a well-known kind of cuisine. Furthermore, there are many diverse vegetarian style dishes in Chinese Buddhist monasteries, like Lingyin Temple in Hangzhou, Shaolin Monastery in Henan, Jade Buddha Temple in Shanghai, Daming Temple in Yangzhou and many other monasteries. Master Hsuan Hua, who came to America propagating Buddhism in the 1960s said that: "Chinese vegetarian food and architecture would go first in the whole process of Buddhism propagation internationally." Thus, many people would become vegetarian and go on to live a life of abstaining from killing on account of the great taste and diverse adequate nutrition in vegetarian food, and also begin to explore Buddhist practice.

For more than two thousand years of Chinese history, Buddhism has been in harmony with vegetarian cuisine. The two have strengthened and complemented each other, promoting each other's mutual development. Vegetarian traditions and culture have become a guarantee of Buddhist practice, which enables the Buddha's wisdom and insight to be implemented in practice in ordinary life, helping people to achieve health both physically and mentally, and thus moving toward the liberation of wisdom.

# May All Beings Be Happy

VICKI SEGLIN

My mantra is *all* beings. These two words appear throughout the Buddhist teachings: "May *all* beings be happy." "*All* beings tremble before violence. *All* fear death; *all* love life." "…Cultivate a boundless love for *all* beings." "So may I become sustenance in every way for sentient beings to the limits of space, until *all* have attained nirvana." "…to nourish our ideal of serving *all* living beings."

It's that *all* that grabs me and speaks to my heart. I have never heard or read a traditional Buddhist teaching that referred to only some beings, or only to human beings. Repeatedly, and pointedly, we are asked to consider all beings as our brothers and sisters, and protect them as we would protect our child. Yet, this basic and clear teaching is often ignored, and the word "human" seems to be silently added, so we can continue to ignore the suffering, at human hands, of our companions on this Earth.

I understand that the path to a vegan lifestyle can be a difficult transformation; my journey has certainly been a winding road that was longer than expected. It has been a gradual and convoluted voyage, and yet now it feels comfortable, makes sense to me, and evokes joy. I slid into Buddhism with an ease I never would have predicted. However, slowly, and with more difficulty, the strong yearning to lead a vegan lifestyle asserted itself and changed my life.

Raised by an Irish/English Catholic mother and a Latvian/Czech Jewish father, it seemed inevitable that neither religion would truly take root. The requirement of the Church, in order for my parents to be married by a priest as my mother desired, was that their children would be raised as Catholics. While I maintain elements of both Judaism and Catholicism in my life, the remnants have been more cultural than spiritual. When I went to college, I quickly left my Catholic mass, communion, and confession behind. Though I would describe myself in those days as kind, and capable of awe and wonder, these were not embedded in any specific spiritual path. I recognized that I was lacking a spiritual community and tradition to help guide and sustain me.

Soon after college, in the mid to late 1970's, my best friend, an animal lover and advocate as I believed myself to be, announced that she and her husband were now vegetarians. This was new and exotic, and I joined them in the adventure. There was little in the culture at the time to support this, so although it made sense to me, and I recognized viscerally that eating animals was the opposite of loving them, my friends and I had entered relatively uncharted territory, figuring out what we could eat. We knew nothing, but we forged ahead, making up recipes, buying the few available alternatives such as vegetarian (not vegan!) sausages, and wondering about tofu, and what to do with this mysterious white blob.

Around 1990, a friend of mine told me she was attending a *sangha* (spiritual community) in the tradition of the Vietnamese Buddhist Zen Master and peace activist, Thich Nhat Hanh, also affectionately referred to as Thay, the Vietnamese word for teacher. This meant nothing to me. I mentally filed away the information, but with little interest. And then one day, in the midst of wondering which spiritual path might speak to me, I was in a small feminist bookstore, and Thay's book, *The Miracle of Mindfulness*, caught my eye. Reading it was revelatory and I realized that I could "do" this mindfulness, this practice of meditation and path of compassion. I already "believed" in these without having named them. I felt drawn to this path without having to convince myself or deny parts of myself. I felt happy simply reading his teachings.

Synchronistically, Thay was coming to Chicago shortly after I discovered his book, and I was able to be at an early retreat, with a small group of other practitioners and curious newcomers, to begin my journey. During the retreat, I experienced the joyful and wise qualities of Thay and his monks and nuns, the strength of their practice of mindfulness, and their capacity to look deeply into what we experience, practicing compassion as a way to a happier life and a more just society. Immediately afterward, I joined a local *sangha* and became dedicated to Thay as a teacher on the path of compassion as explained by the Buddha. Thay had been clear that we must, in addition to personal practice and study, get off our cushions, engage in the world as people dedicated to kindness and justice, and participate in a community of like-minded people to support this deceptively "simple" practice.

While still a student of Buddhism, I found the path of veganism to be more complex and challenging. At some point, I recognized that in addition to not eating animals, I was called to stop wearing them in the form of leather shoes, wool jackets, and silk blouses. I allowed what I already owned to wear out naturally and sought out alternatives, which didn't exist in abundance as they do now. We might think this would be obvious: that wearing animals is also abusive to them, but this is how our brains work. As a psychologist, I am aware that we can easily carry opposing views and refuse to acknowledge obvious discrepancies, and be unable to see things if it feels too challenging. Positive transformation is often resisted! Mindfulness practice helped me sit with the conflicting and sometimes painful feelings that arose as I made the necessary changes, and also helped me be patient with those who were hostile to my becoming a vegan, and to be patient with myself when I judged that I was changing too slowly.

I continued attending sangha meetings, going to retreats, studying, and reading and listening to Dharma talks. I became more of an animal rights activist, working with local groups on various issues, such as ending vivisection experiments at a local university, as well as supporting campaigns like Fur Free Friday demonstrations and pigeon shoot protests. Yet, I continued to eat eggs, drink milk, and order Chicago deep-dish pizzas.

Gradually, through reading, viewing videos, and through meditating on the reality of the animals' lives, my understanding deepened, as did my wish to protect all beings. I gradually freed myself from the fantasy, fed by advertising and cultural propaganda, that dairy, eggs, and cheese don't require killing and mistreating animals.

My mother had been born and raised in a rural town in northwest Iowa, and when we would visit every summer, I could see the cows and the pigs freely roaming in the fields and assumed they must be having a fine life, enjoying the sunshine and living a natural lifespan. Relatives in New Hampshire owned a dairy farm and every cow had a name, so how could they do anything cruel to them? But in educating myself about the actual state of affairs in animal agriculture, for example, the forced impregnations of dairy cows, the killing of the baby calves, the hyper-confinement of hens and other animals, and the many even more abusive standard practices, I realized I could no longer support this violence, nor close my eyes concerning what I was eating.

However, becoming a vegan turned out to be unexpectedly difficult. I struggled with it, decreasing the amount of dairy and eggs I ate, but having trouble eliminating them completely from my diet. I wanted to, desperately, but in those days, veganism was not as recognized in the mainstream culture as it is now; there was little social support and fewer options. I also resisted the changes this would create in my life and in my relationships. Nevertheless, I persisted.

There were two definitive events that helped me finally make the transition. One was finding out that some digestive issues I was having were due to my being allergic to dairy products and eggs. If I believe in a benevolent energy in the universe, it was helping me with this transition to veganism. Milk, eggs, ice cream…gone. The second event involved cheese. For several years, I had occasional Dairy Days, not very often, and usually connected to a birthday party, for example, when I craved a piece of cake. But the real problem was cheese. Every few months, I would "have to have" a Chicago pizza. These days, anyone can get vegan Chicago pizzas, but nothing like this existed until fairly recently. The real attraction was the cheese. Why was it so hard to let go of this? I understood that I didn't have to be perfect; that would be impossible. I also knew that this vegan choice I was making was not about me; it was about the animals and their suffering. My decisions make a difference in the world. So I continued to try.

Fortunately, my friend and colleague, John Bussineau, wrote his first book, *The Buddha, The Vegan and You*. His book taught me a lot, even given my many years of educating myself on the issues. His section on "Analytical Antidote for Cheese," detailing how to use a Tibetan form of analytical meditation to help us resist the "pull" of cheese, along with one of the most effective and graphic descriptions of how buying and eating cheese harms other living beings, combined with the knowledge that cheese was physiologically addictive, was enough to stop the madness. Dairy Days became a relic of the past, and I am grateful for that. Compassion is lighter to carry than cruelty.

Throughout this journey to veganism, I was also learning more about integrating the Buddha's teachings into my daily life. I continued to participate in the local *sangha*, eventually becoming ordained as a lay member of Thay's Order of Interbeing. For me, this was a statement that I was publicly committing to living according to the Bodhisattva Vows and the Fourteen Mindfulness Trainings. The Bodhisattva Vows are inextricably linked to my vegan vows. How can I not take the "all beings" phrase seriously as an integral part of my Buddhist practice?

There have been challenges on this path, such as learning to handle strong emotions with equanimity, and judgments that arise without warning, as well as struggling to respond compassionately to certain people. However, being vegan is no longer a struggle or a challenge. Some have suggested I might have been a cow in a previous life; I will not rule this out!

I feel fortunate that my teacher, Thay, is forthright about the importance of compassion for animals, unlike numerous Buddhist and spiritual teachers. In public talks, he has discussed the suffering of animals, and the ways in which our knowledge of this can help us stop buying and eating their flesh, their children, and their "products." He says, "To be vegan is not perfect, but it helps to reduce the suffering of animals."

I am grateful for the existence of Dharma Voices for Animals, an international group dedicated to educating people, particularly those in the Buddhist community, about animal abuse and the vegan lifestyle. This coming together of the Buddhist and vegan paths is both essential and inevitable, and can help sustain those of us who may feel isolated as vegans and animal advocates, even within our Buddhist communities.

When someone challenges me or implies that I am being extreme for refraining from killing animals, I find it helpful to remember the Mindfulness Trainings, including:

> We are committed not to kill and not to let others kill. We will not support any act of killing in the world, in our thinking, or in our way of life.

> We will practice loving kindness by working for the happiness of people, animals, plants, and minerals.

Increasingly, the Buddhist and the vegan paths feel like two aspects of one interconnected path, each leading back to the other, and providing guidance and encouragement for each other. They are both sources of joy, creative challenge, and harmony. May *all* beings be joyful and live in comfort and ease, free from fear. This is within reach, if we allow our habit energies to be transformed, include our non-human brothers and sisters into our circle of compassion, and continue to challenge ourselves to live in ways that decrease suffering for *all* beings.

# Birthday Crashing and Spiritual Awakening

PAUL TARCHICHI (BROTHER PROMISE)

## Franck's birthday

"Franck's inviting us to his birthday!" my sister said. "Would you like to go?"

I am a vegan monk and my friend Franck is a butcher.

"Sure," I said.

Franck must have heard I was in Paris for a few days, visiting my family before flying to a monastery in New York. My sister and I knocked on his door and he greeted us with a smile. I was happy to see him again— it had been many years. Franck is a nice guy, with a quick wit and a great sense of humor. The atmosphere was peaceful and we mingled easily with the other guests.

"Dinner is ready!" His wife announced. We all sat down at the table, watching her lovingly place fragrant, carefully prepared dishes on the table: basmati rice, ratatouille, and . . . chicken! As fate would have it, the chicken dish was placed right in front of me.

"Chicken, anyone?" I asked.

Many passed their plates and I happily served them.

As for me, I chose the rice and vegetables.

"You're not having chicken?" one guest asked.

"No, thank you...but it looks delicious!" I politely answered.

"Are you vegan?" another inquired.

"Yes," I nodded.

I am a happy vegan. As far as I know, going vegan is the number one thing we can do for our health, for the animals, and for the planet. I sometimes share with others about the benefits of veganism, when the moment is right. That particular afternoon, however, I just wanted to *connect* with everyone. I wanted to feel comfortable with them, just as they were. I also wanted to create conditions for them to feel safe and comfortable with me. I was not particularly keen on getting offended, or seeing others getting offended by me being offended at them "not seeing how offensive the whole thing was" (if that makes sense).

I sincerely did not wish to see Franck's birthday dinner crashed by a self-invited vegan campaign. Nevertheless, it still happened.

A few seats away from me, two guests set out to speak animatedly about the animals' suffering, and about how wrong it was to consume meat. The atmosphere quickly became tense, and several guests were showing signs of discomfort. It seemed we were all worried about how Franck would react.

"I know . . ." he said.

The room silenced and everyone was all ears. Franck then proceeded to talk in even more depth about the suffering of the animals, and the cruelty of an industry he knew all too well. He said he had inherited the profession from his father. He said the industry wasn't what it used to be. He said he had been looking for ways to change career for years, because he didn't believe it would ever be possible for him to practice his job with a clear conscience.

## Listening deeply

In Buddhism, we learn about the practice of deep listening. To listen deeply to someone, with a calm and open mind, without judging or reacting, can be very healing, not only for the one who speaks, but also for the listener. Deep listening allows us to open our hearts to others' realities, and to understand them better.

If we were to take time to listen, as individuals and as a society, we would quickly realize that indeed, Franck is not the only one suffering in the animal farming industry.

According to Human Rights Watch, "Meatpacking is the most dangerous factory job in America."[1] Factory farm workers suffer high injury rates, due to a combination of strenuous hours, time pressure, heavy lifting, and handling of sharp knives and other dangerous equipment.[2] They routinely inhale hazardous levels of particulate matter (from animal dander, feathers, and so on), ammonia (urine) and hydrogen sulfide gases (manure).[3] However, "The worst thing, worse than the physical danger," said one slaughterhouse worker, "is the emotional toll... Pigs down on the kill floor have come up and nuzzled me like a puppy. Two minutes later I had to kill them..."[4] The psychological damage inflicted by the job is well documented.[5] According to statistics, the mere presence of a slaughterhouse in a community guarantees a drastic increase in alcoholism, violence, domestic abuse, child abuse and suicide.[6]

Listening can be difficult—even overwhelming at times—but it is the *one and only way* for us to develop more understanding and compassion. To open our hearts and listen propels us to live more responsibly, more beautifully, more meaningfully. We are 7.5 billion people on Earth, and *every year we kill for consumption 70 billion land animals*[7] *and 2.7 trillion sea animals.*[8]

If we were to listen deeply enough, we would hear the cries of these animals. Behind the alluring advertising, behind the closed walls of the farms and slaughterhouses, stand painful realities. Females are routinely raped, i.e., artificially inseminated. Many dairy calves are hyperconfined, forced into anemia, and killed at just one to five months old for veal meat. Male chicks, who cannot lay eggs or be sold for meat, are killed at birth. Animals are routinely castrated, their tails cut, horns cut, ears notched, teeth clipped, and beaks and toes sliced off, all without anesthesia. They are compelled to live in the filthiest conditions, often literally on top of each other, without ever seeing the light of day.[9]

It is difficult for us to connect with the inner worlds of these living, feeling, breathing creatures. We can pet our companion animals, love them, feed them, play with them, share our joys and sorrows with them, and shed tears when their time comes. We can feel elated when looking at birds soaring in the air. We can be moved by the beauty of wildlife. We can be struck by the preciousness of life. Yet, when it comes to certain animals that we have, as a society, labeled as "items of consumption," we can also be quick to disconnect.

To be kept alive in what are often extremely unsanitary conditions, animals are fed enormous quantities of antibiotics. The meat industry has thus become one of the driving forces worldwide behind the development of antibiotic resistance in human disease-causing bacteria.[10] Additionally, to produce more meat at a faster pace, young animals are injected with strong growth hormones. All of those chemicals will not only be found in the flesh, eggs and milk that people consume, but will also be released into the environment.[11] The gases, urine, and manure produced by the animals also have a significant negative impact on ecosystems.[12] Most people don't realize that animal agriculture is the leading source of greenhouse gas emissions worldwide.[13] The United Nations has warned us: "A global shift towards a vegan diet is vital to save the world from the worst impacts of climate change."[14]

*Feeding the world's billions of farm animals requires tremendous amounts of water, grains, and land, making animal farming one of the worst strategies for resource management.* Worldwide, animal agriculture is responsible for twenty to thirty percent of all fresh water consumption[15] and for at least fifty percent of grain consumption.[16] Livestock covers forty-five percent of the earth's total land.[17] Livestock and their feed crops are the leading cause of rain forest destruction.[18] Providing for a meat-eater requires six times more land than for a vegetarian; providing for a vegetarian still requires three times more land than for a vegan![19] Animal agriculture is also the leading cause of ocean dead zones[20] and, if the world keeps fishing at its current pace, scientists expect the oceans to be empty of fish by 2048.[21]

In a world where human population is quickly rising and natural resources are becoming ever scarcer, isn't it time to reconsider our dietary paradigm?

### A clever, healthy consumer

As consumers, we tend to see ourselves at the end of the production chain. The meat, fish, eggs and dairy products are already available at the supermarket. The animal has already been killed. The damage has already been done. This is true, but it's only *half* of the truth. The other half is that, whenever we pay for those products, we financially support the animal farming industry and propel that industry to continue. Therefore, as consumers, we are not only at the end of the production chain, but also at the beginning. We decide.

Now, here is the great news: *studies show that choosing a whole food, plant-based diet is a remarkably effective way to improve our health.* Vegans tend to live longer, healthier lives,[22] with lower rates of heart disease, cancer, respiratory diseases, Alzheimer's, diabetes, high blood pressure, obesity, and other dreaded diseases of our time. Not only that, but *in many cases, a whole food, plant-based diet can help reverse these ailments.*[23] [24] [25]

Plants are perfect sources of protein and calcium and are processed more easily by our bodies than animal-sourced protein and calcium. In addition, they do not come with the cholesterol, saturated fats, and other harmful substances found in animal products. A vegan diet, with a variety of greens, vegetables, fruits, legumes, whole grains, nuts and seeds, herbs and spices, complemented with a B12 supplement,[26] provides us with all the fiber, vitamins, minerals, antioxidants, and other nutrients that we need.

### The Four Noble Vegan Truths

At the core of Buddhist philosophy is the teaching on the Four Noble Truths: suffering, the causes of suffering, happiness and healing, and the path to happiness and healing. The task of a Buddhist practitioner is not to intellectually approve of those truths, but to *awaken* to them, in herself and in the world she lives in. This is essential.

Sickness is suffering. Torture and killing is suffering. The depletion of natural resources is suffering. As Buddhist practitioners, we are called to open our eyes, hearts and minds to these realities. This is the first step. The second step is to look deeply and identify the main cause of these sufferings, namely our daily dietary food choices. The third is to realize that it is possible to put an end to this suffering. Going vegan decreases our chances of getting sick, puts an end to the torture and killing, and the unnecessary depletion of natural resources. Our last task is to engage on the path of healing and happiness, the path of *veganism*.

The role of a Buddhist community, like the role of any spiritual community, is to cultivate love in action. Love is not something abstract. It is a practice, and this practice requires understanding. As a nun, monk, or lay practitioner, *to learn about Buddhism is not enough*. We also need to learn about the world we live in, so as to express our spirituality in a way that is concrete and relevant.

To *only* learn about Buddhism is actually harmful to Buddhism. Buddhism is about the present moment, and about awakening to who we are, to the life that surrounds us. Life itself is the object of our meditation and the field of our experience. Life itself is the object of our love.

We need to look at our real problems, such as our health issues, our feelings of alienation, our feelings of purposelessness, or our lack of connection. We are called to face the real situation of our society, the animals, and our planet. We need to use our energy of mindfulness, our calmness, curiosity, open-mindedness, and scientific spirit to search for solutions: *solutions we can apply*.

## Buddhism: a short (although still boring) history

For better or for worse, the Buddhist community is steeped in a long history of tradition, which began 2600 years ago in India. At that time, Siddhartha Gautama (the Buddha) and his monastic disciples were all mendicants. Going from house to house every day to beg for food, they practiced humility, acceptance, and gratitude. Begging allowed them to be in touch with lay people, to understand them better and offer spiritual guidance.

> *All beings fear pain.*
> *All beings fear death.*
> *Empathize with them.*
> *Do not kill, and do not cause others to kill.*[27]

The Buddha encouraged everyone to abstain from taking life, so as to "free countless beings from danger, oppression,

*Buddhism & Veganism*

and animosity."[28] He instructed his lay disciples to adopt a right livelihood, not engaging in the trade of meat.[29] He said that capturing and killing an animal creates suffering for the animal and negative karma for ourselves.[30] He instructed his monastic disciples to never take part in animal ritual sacrifices[31] and, when going on their daily alms round, to never accept the flesh of an animal when they had seen the animal being killed for them, heard that the animal had been killed for them, or even *suspected* that the animal *might* have been killed for them.[32]

However strong this policy may seem, it still left room for a last case scenario: the case in which a family had already cooked their non-vegetarian meal and wanted to share it with the monks and nuns. In that case, the begging monk or nun could accept the offering. Already at that time, this gesture attracted criticism.[33] To put things into context, one should remember that monks and nuns often traveled to share the Dhamma with strangers, and that their training emphasized acceptance and humility.[34] With monastics often begging by the hundreds, it would most likely have been judged "too demanding" for the Sangha to ask for special vegan meals to be cooked for them every day.

From these historical facts, we might infer that although the Buddhist monks and nuns preferred a plant-based diet, which was more in accordance with their vows of compassion, they accepted shares of meals cooked by non-vegetarian families, so as not to offend them and to give them a chance to learn about Dharma. "Some day," they might have wished, "no one will offer us meat, and we will be able to only eat vegetarian food."[35] Before passing away, the Buddha told Ānanda (his personal attendant and one of his most senior disciples) that although the monastic Sangha should keep its core precepts, it could get rid of the minor ones as seen fit.[36] Changing the monastic rules is nothing new. The Buddha and his Sangha created the precepts as they went along, regularly editing some, even dropping others. To do so, we need to understand what these precepts are

148

about: *compassion*. After the Buddha's passing, some traditions updated their precepts to implement mandatory vegetarianism. This was greatly facilitated by the fact that many communities settled in one place and began cooking (and often growing) their own food.

## Connecting

In the community I belong to, which is the Plum Village community, our precepts require us to be vegetarians, but not vegans. In 2006, our teacher, Zen master Thich Nhat Hanh, asked us to go vegan. Although we have been making progress towards a completely vegan diet, we are not there yet, both as a community and as individuals. Consuming eggs, milk and dairy is still, technically, not an infraction of our monastic code. One day, I hope it will be.

I sometimes feel sad and disappointed when I see a brother or sister buying or consuming eggs and dairy products, but I practice patience. I take care of my feelings, remembering that I haven't always been a vegan myself! I remember that, although I might practice better than they do in this particular area, there are many other areas in which they practice better than I. I remember that the purpose of becoming vegan is to bring more compassion into my life, not more pride and separation. Above all, I remind myself that *I do not want to wait for everyone to be like me to be his or her friend.*

I practice taking care of myself first. I practice enjoying being a vegan. I keep learning about veganism and I try to cultivate *good relationships*. I keep in my heart the words of wisdom I received from an elder brother many years ago: "When you see someone doing something you don't approve of, don't be too quick to judge, and don't be too quick to reprimand. If you don't have a good relationship with them, you might cause them to feel hurt, to react strongly and to not want to listen to what you have to say. In other words: don't correct... connect!"

### Planting seeds

I want to maintain good connections with others, and only when I have enough acceptance and understanding for them, only when the time is ripe, do I want to share my suggestions. In the monastery where I live now, Blue Cliff Monastery in New York State, I recently gave a talk titled "Why vegan?"[37] I was happy to learn that following this talk, several members of my community became fully vegan (until the time of this writing, at least!)

Choosing vegan options for myself, when other options are available, is making a statement and opening possibilities for others. We teach by our actions.

People who come to our practice centers know that vegan food can be delicious. One day, I learned that many young friends wanted to go vegan but didn't know how to cook. This prompted me to organize a vegan cooking workshop. The following Sunday, we went to the market together, bought a variety of fresh produce, and cooked many delicious dishes. We had so much fun! If you would like to help family and friends discover the joy of plant-based eating, a nice and polite way is to invite them for a delicious and flavorful dinner, either at home or in a vegan restaurant.

Another important, simple and effective way to spread the word of veganism is through social media. I share vegan clips quite regularly on my Facebook page, but *spaced* with other useful content that may still, by the way, include clips of funny, cute animals, which I hope will water the seeds of joy and tenderness in my friends! I avoid sharing massively in one go and, above all, I do not *only* share about veganism. No, I don't want my friends to block me! And yes, I have been meditating on this.

If I had to summarize in one sentence what I have learned from Buddhist practice, it would probably be this: "I can always contribute, but I can never control." I am one of the many conditions co-creating all the people I meet. Because I am one of them, I can always contribute, and I want to do so beautifully.

But because I am *only* one of those many conditions, I can never fully control anyone or anything. Remembering this helps me to connect to my own creative power while, at the same time, preserving my sanity and peace of mind.

I want to sow seeds in people's hearts, and I try to do so peacefully and skillfully. Whether these seeds will sprout and bear fruit or not depends on the conditions. When my sharing seems to have no effect, I find consolation in the fact that I have planted a seed. I remember that the seed is still there, waiting for conditions to manifest, and one day, when I least expect it, it might surprise me by growing into a strong and beautiful plant.

### Caring for our "Francks"

The animals need our compassion; this is essential and undeniable but our "Francks" deserve it too.

There are many ways to help those working in the animal farming industry. As individuals, we can learn to be their good friends. Buddhist practice can help. With mindful breathing, we can better handle our emotions. We can slowly move past the limiting labels of "victims" and "perpetrators" and "good" and "evil." We can begin to understand their past, social conditioning, and day-to-day realities. We can begin to love. Love brings us more peace. Love gives them a chance to bloom as human beings, and a human being who has fully bloomed cannot kill anymore.

As a society, we can learn to make better choices—locally, regionally, and nationally. It has already been done, and it can be done again.[38] We can inform. We can educate. We can unlock governmental funds for animal farmers to grow grains, fruits and vegetables. To protect the physical and mental health of our citizens is not only a noble moral endeavor, it is also a wise economic investment. A healthy nation spends less on health care, less on prisons, and is more creative and productive.

## In summary

If you are a Buddhist, I would like to suggest to you: Going vegan will help you better realize your spiritual ideals. Going vegan is good for your health, the animals, the Earth, and future generations. Going vegan can help you become a better role model for society. Please consider.

If you are already vegan, please remember: This is about compassion... and everyone needs and deserves compassion. Just like a good Buddhist needs non-Buddhist friends, a good vegan needs non-vegan friends. So please, *connect.*

References:
1.  "Blood, Sweat and Fear: Workers' Rights in U.S. Meat and Poultry Plants." *Human Rights Watch Report*, January 2005
2.  "Workplace Safety and Health: Safety in the Meat and Poultry Industry, while Improving, Could Be Further Strengthened." A report by the Government Accountability Office. 2005.
3.  "Concentrated Animal Feedlot Operations (CAFOs) Chemicals Associated with Air Emissions." Prepared by the CAFO subcommittee of the Michigan Department of Environmental Quality (MDEQ) Toxics Steering Group (TSG). 2006.
4.  *Slaughterhouse: The Shocking Story of Greed, Neglect, and Inhumane Treatment Inside the U.S. Meat Industry*, by Gail A. Eisnitz.
5.  Dillard, Jennifer. "A Slaughterhouse Nightmare: Psychological Harm Suffered by Slaughterhouse Employees and the Possibility of Redress through Legal Reform." *Georgetown Journal on Poverty Law & Policy*, forthcoming.
6.  "Slaughterhouses and Increased Crime Rates: An Empirical Analysis of the Spillover From "The Jungle" Into the Surrounding Community," by Amy J. Fitzgerald, University of Windsor, Linda Kalof, Michigan State University, and Thomas Dietz, Michigan State University. *Organization & Environment*, June 2009.
7.  "Factory Farms," A Well Fed World
8.  Mood, A. & Brooke, P. "Estimating the Number of Fish Caught in Global Fishing Each Year," July 2010.
9.  *A Plea for the Animals: The Moral, Philosophical, and Evolutionary Imperative to Treat All Beings with Compassion*, by Matthieu Ricard.
10. *Food Animals and Antimicrobials: Impacts on Human Health*, Bonnie M. Marshall, Stuart B. Levy
11. "Animal Agriculture & Climate Change," The Humane Society of the United States. Web Accessed April 18, 2015.
12. "Pollution from Giant Livestock Farms Threatens Public Health," Natural Resources Defense Council. Web Accessed April 18, 2015.
13. "Livestock and Climate Change: What if the key actors in climate change are...cows, pigs and chickens?" Goodland, Robert & Anhang, Jeff. *WorldWatch*, November/December 2009.
14. June 2010 report from the United Nations Environment Programme (UNEP).
15. Mekonnen, Mesfin M. & Hoekstra, Arjen Y. "A Global Assessment of the Water Footprint of Farm Animal Products." *Ecosystems* (2012) 15: 401-415.
16. "Executive Summary: Feed Supply," Food and Agriculture Organization of the United Nations.

17. Thornton, Phillip, et al., "Livestock and climate change," *Livestock Xchange*. International Livestock Research Institute, November 2011.
18. Butler, Rhett. "Cattle Ranching's Impact on the Rainforest." Mongabay.com. July 2012 ; Veiga, J.B., et al. *Cattle Ranching in the Amazon Rainforest*. UN: Food and Agriculture Organization.
19. Robbins, John. *Diet for a New America*, StillPoint Publishing, 1987, p. 352
20. "What Causes Ocean 'Dead Zones'?" *Scientific American*
21. "Impacts of biodiversity loss on ocean ecosystem services." Worm, Boris; Barbier, Edward B.
22. *Beyond Meatless, the Health Effects of Vegan Diets: Findings from the Adventist Cohorts*, by Lap Tai Le and Joan Sabaté.
23. *The China Study: Revised and Expanded Edition: The Most Comprehensive Study of Nutrition Ever Conducted and the Startling Implications for Diet, Weight Loss, and Long-Term Health*, by T. Colin Campbell and M.D. Thomas M. Campbell II.
24. *How Not to Die: Discover the Foods Scientifically Proven to Prevent and Reverse Disease*, by Michael Greger and Gene Stone.
25. http://nutritionfacts.org
26. It is not just most vegans who are deficient in B12, but most meat eaters are, too.
27. *Dhammapada*, verse 129
28. *Abhisanda Sutta* - AN 8.39
29. *Vanijja Sutta* - AN 5.177
30. *Jivaka Sutta* - MN 55
31. *Brahmajāla Sutta* - DN1
32. *Bhikkhu Pātimokkha*, M.I,369
33. *Jivaka Sutta* - MN 55
34. *Ariyavamsa Sutta* - AN 4.28
35. *Old Path White Clouds*, Thich Nhat Hanh. chapter 58.
36. *Mahāparinibbāna Sutta* - DN.16.
37. https://youtu.be/ZQiJ6sSPw1A.
38. Finland is a good example. https://www.pritikin.com/your-health/health-benefits/reverse-heart-disease/252-heart-disease-deaths-plunge-75.html

# Waking Up with Each Bite: Contemplations for Meals

ANDREW BEAR

~~~~~~~~~~~~~~~~~~~~~~~~~~~~~~~~~~~~~~~~~~~~~~~~~~~~~~~~~~~~~~~

Waking up. Waking up is said to be the vocation of sincere followers of the Buddha. We recall that the word, "Buddha" means "the awakened one." A Buddha is not a transcendent being, a celestial deity, or a god, but a human being who is awake. The teachings of the Buddha emphasize waking up. We might ask, "awakening to what?"

Since meeting my teacher, Thich Nhat Hanh, in 1991, I feel I've been on a journey of awakening. This journey is a path, not a final destination, and one of the most notable ways my life has changed is in my practice of eating. Eating might not be the first thing that comes to mind when we think of Buddhist practice. We may perhaps envision a person meditating under a tree, or sitting on a cushion in a temple, or a monk chanting rituals. For me, eating—the daily, mundane act of eating—embodies my path of waking up.

### Beginning to Awaken

About ten years after first meeting Thich Nhat Hanh, I attended a talk that he gave two days after 9/11. My heart was rattled and heavy, and I was fearful about how my country, the United States, would respond to the attack. I was looking forward to words of comfort from "Thay" as he is called by his students. While I found comfort and peace in Thay's serene and potent presence, he spoke about a not-very-comforting sutra called, "The Discourse on the Son's Flesh."

> [The Buddha] used the example of a young couple who wanted to flee their country and to live in another country. The young couple brought their little boy with them and a quantity of food with them. But halfway through the desert they ran out of food. They knew that they were going to die. After much debate they decided to kill the little boy and to eat his flesh. The title of the sutra is, *The Son's Flesh*. They killed the little boy and they ate one piece of that flesh and they preserved the rest on their shoulders for the sun to dry. Every time they ate a piece of flesh of their son they asked the question, "Where is our beloved son now? Where are you, our beloved son?" They beat their chests and they pulled their hair. They suffered tremendously. But finally they were able to cross the desert and enter the other country.

The Buddha turned to his monks and asked, 'Dear friends, do you think the couple enjoyed eating the flesh of their son?' And the monks said, 'No, how could anyone enjoy eating the flesh of their own son?' The Buddha said, 'If we do not consume mindfully we are eating the flesh of our own son or daughter.'

Thay then shared statistics about animal agriculture—its impact on land use, water, pollution, and deforestation. He said that mindfulness will help us see the violence in our food, and that we are essentially eating our father, our mother, our children, and the Earth. The practice of mindfulness helps us see the violence in the food we produce and eat. Thay said, "We should learn to eat together in such a way that compassion can remain in our hearts."

I began to awaken. I gave up eating meat at this talk.

The next year I was invited to dinner by a friend who lived out in the country. My friend learned that I had never had tri-tip, a specific cut of meat from a cow, and insisted I try it; I decided to be a gracious guest and eat some. After the dinner, however, I felt bad for eating the flesh of a cow, and went outside by myself. I sat down on a patio chair, next to his neighbor's fence. The neighbor was a rancher, I found out, as a cow came over to the fence and started looking at me. Soon, the whole herd of cows came over, about forty of them. They were all looking directly at me and started mooing! It was a striking experience, and I had the feeling that they knew that I had just eaten one of their kind. I went over to the fence, stroked a few of the cows on the sides of their heads, and told them, "I'm sorry. I promise I will never eat your people again." I have kept this promise.

It took me about another eight years before I became vegan. Again, it was the influence of Thich Nhat Hanh. I read what became known as "The Blue Cliff Letter," which Thay wrote in 2007 at the Blue Cliff monastery in New York State. He detailed the effects of animal agriculture, and wrote,

"Thầy believes that it is not so difficult to stop eating meat, when we know that we are saving the planet by doing so. We only need to be vegetarian, and we can already save the earth. Being vegetarian here also means that we do not consume dairy and egg products, because they are products of the meat industry. If we stop consuming, they will stop producing. Only collective awakening can create enough determination for action."

I remember reading this letter near the end of 2009, and decided to begin a vegan lifestyle on New Year's Day 2010. My journey of awakening continued.

## Contemplations Before Eating

"Looking deeply" is a core practice and teaching in Thich Nhat Hanh's tradition. "Looking deeply" is another way of translating the Pali word, "Vipassana," which is often translated as "Insight."

One application of the practice of looking deeply is the chant that many Buddhist traditions recite before meals. This chant is known as the Five Contemplations Before Eating. If we practice the Five Contemplations Before Eating, they will support us as we look deeply at our food and eat with mindfulness and compassion. In Thich Nhat Hanh's tradition, the Contemplations Before Eating are:

This food is a gift of the earth, the sky, numerous living beings, and much hard and loving work.

May we eat with mindfulness and gratitude so as to be worthy to receive this food.

May we recognize and transform unwholesome mental formations, especially our greed and learn to eat with moderation.

May we keep our compassion alive by eating in such a way that reduces the suffering of living beings, stops contributing to climate change, and heals and preserves our precious planet.

We accept this food so that we may nurture our brotherhood and sisterhood, build our *sangha*, and nourish our ideal of serving all living beings.

The first and fourth of the contemplations are the most alive in my practice, and have had the greatest impact in my life.

### Food as Ambassador of the Cosmos

The first contemplation is, "This food is a gift of the earth, the sky, numerous living beings, and much hard and loving work." This first contemplation invites us to look deeply and contemplate our food with the insight of interbeing. "Interbeing" is a word coined by Thich Nhat Hanh that conveys the Buddha's teaching that everything is interconnected; nothing exists as an isolated entity.

When I contemplate a spoonful of oatmeal, for example, and practice looking deeply, I can see the oat plant in a field, with its roots in the soil. In the soil, there are many nutrients for the oat plant. There are millions of tiny organisms in the soil. There are mycelium and fungi, as well as decaying organic matter. There are insects and worms that help break down the decaying organic matter and there are countless bacteria. I see this whole community of life in this spoonful of oatmeal.

There are also broken rocks and minerals in the soil, which are taken up by the oat plant. These minerals were once part of ancient stars that exploded billions of years ago, so there are literally stars in our spoon of oatmeal!

As I continue to look deeply, I can envision the oat plant blowing in the wind. I know that oats happen to be wind-pollinated, so there would not be an oat plant without the wind. Because wind is caused by differences in atmospheric pressure, flowing from places of high pressure to low pressure, if I look deeply, I can see the changing pressures of our atmosphere are also in the spoonful of oatmeal.

I can also see clouds and the ocean in the spoonful of oatmeal. When the winds blow over the ocean and cause waves, with spray and whitecaps, tiny droplets of ocean water are thrown up into the atmosphere where some evaporate. As warm air rises, it expands and cools, and water vapor condenses, forming a cloud. Cool air can't hold as much water vapor, so some of the water vapor condenses, attaches to little pieces of dust floating in the air, and forms droplets around the tiny pieces of dust. When these droplets become heavy enough, they will fall to the earth, watering and nourishing the oat plant. So looking deeply, I can see the ocean, clouds and rain in the spoonful of oatmeal.

I can also see the sun in my spoonful of oatmeal. Without the sun, the oat plant would not grow. The light of the sun provides energy that the oat plant uses to live and grow, and gives warmth for the oat plant as well. Continuing to open to the spoonful of oatmeal, I can see the changing of seasons, which influence the planting, growth, and harvesting of the oats. I can see the inclination of the Earth's axis, which is creating the changing seasons. All of this is in the spoonful of oatmeal.

There is also the farmer who planted the oat seed, those who tended the crop and harvested the oat plant. Looking deeply into these farmers, we see all of their ancestors through time, the social and cultural influences that led them to become farmers or field laborers, and perhaps wonder about the lives of those working in the fields. This may bring up questions of economic justice, human migration, and politics.

We are also in the spoonful of oatmeal, because without our desire for oats, which creates the economic incentive to grow them, the oats might not exist.

The seasons, the soil with its billions of living beings, the stars, the sun, the wind, the ocean, the clouds, the floating dust,

the rain, the atmospheric pressure, the farmers and their ancestors, and you and I, are all in that spoonful of oats. If we remove
any of those elements, our spoonful of oats would not exist. This
illustrates the insight of interbeing, an insight that can grow
within us as we practice looking deeply into our food.

As Thich Nhat Hanh says, each bite of food is an "ambassador of the cosmos."

### Food as Ambassador of Suffering

The fourth contemplations before eating is, "May we keep our
compassion alive by eating in such a way that reduces the suffering of living beings, stops contributing to climate change, and
heals and preserves our precious planet." This fourth contemplation invites us to eat in a way that nourishes our compassion and
reduces suffering for living beings and our precious mother Earth.

If, instead of eating oatmeal we are eating an animal product, when we look deeply we will see abuse and suffering. We will
know that humans kill 60 billion farm animals and several trillion fish each year. That means that globally, more than 60,000
living beings are killed *per second* for human consumption. We
can contemplate that and let it sink in. That's 60,000 living beings now…now…now…and now.

There is a saying, "If slaughterhouses had glass walls,
everyone would be vegetarian." The suffering of farm animals,
however, starts at their birth.

Looking deeply, we will know that 99 percent of chickens
raised in the United States are raised in windowless sheds that
hold tens of thousands of birds each. Because they are forced to
breathe ammonia and particulate matter from feces all day long,
they often suffer serious health problems, including chronic respiratory illnesses and bacterial infections.

We will also see that chickens are bred to grow much
faster and larger than normal. The average chicken today is four
times larger than a chicken bred in the 1950s. Many chickens

are crippled, unable to stand or walk, because their legs cannot support the weight of their bodies.

Chickens also have their sensitive beaks cut off with hot blades, without painkillers, when they are one to ten days old, so they won't peck each other because of frustration from their intense confinement. Some of these birds will starve to death, because the pain from being "de-beaked" makes eating too painful.

In looking deeply at a piece of chicken flesh, we will see intense emotional suffering due to overcrowding. For example, how does it feel to be in a packed elevator with very little room to move? I ride an elevator daily at my workplace in an older building, so the elevators stop working fairly often. Every time I get on the elevator I am taking a risk and I often think about what it would be like to be stuck in a crowded elevator. Imagine being confined in a crowded elevator for fifteen minutes... or one hour...or one whole day. Now imagine being confined to that elevator for your entire life, crammed with so many people you could barely turn around, breathing in urine and feces. I don't know about you, but I imagine that I would go insane with suffering.

Marketing chickens as "cage free" and "free range" often gives people the impression that the chickens had an enjoyable life, but these terms are unfortunately little more than marketing gimmicks. "Cage free" operations force intense crowding onto chickens, but without cages. In other words, a cage-free chicken will still be raised in a shed with tens of thousands of other oversized, de-beaked chickens who never see the light of day, without the ability to move about, breathing in ammonia-drenched air with fecal waste.

"Free range" means that the chickens technically have access to a door that would enable the birds to go outside for a portion of the day, but often due to intense overcrowding, virtually none the birds will ever experience sunshine and fresh air their entire lives.

Many people who eat eggs assume that eggs are a fairly harmless animal product. If one looks deeply at an egg, however, one will see even more abusive conditions than those in which chickens are raised for meat, including intense crowding and debeaking. In nature, hens will lay twelve to fifteen eggs per year, and only during breeding season. In the egg industry, hens have been bred to lay between 250 and 300 eggs per year, and their food intake and lighting conditions are manipulated to increase productivity. After about 18 to 24 months, as hens' egg-laying productivity declines, these "spent" hens will be sent to slaughter. As a means of comparison, in their native jungle habitat, hens live between ten and fifteen years and play a vital role in the symbiosis of their native forest community.

Looking more deeply, we will see that because male chicks are worthless to the egg industry, they are either thrown into plastic bags and suffocated, or thrown into grinders alive.

The egg industry uses the same deceptive advertising as the "broiler chickens" raised for meat. For example, a prominent egg farm that sells "organic" and "free range" eggs requested and received a waiver to keep their hens inside to supposedly protect them from weather, disease, and predators. Their hens never see the light of day, but they are still allowed to advertise them as "free range." The owner of this company said, in defense, that although people expect that free range hens all have access to the outdoors, "That doesn't happen. That doesn't happen anywhere."

This fourth meal contemplation invites us to keep our compassion alive and encourages us to make an effort to reduce suffering of all living beings. If we look deeply at our food, and we are subsidizing and eating any animal product, we will see suffering and violence.

It is true that it is impossible to be completely nonviolent, and that all eating involves killing. There are microorganisms that we kill when we boil water. Plants are killed in a vegan diet, along with insects and other animals in many agricultural practices. We may not be able to be one hundred percent nonviolent, but we can make it a practice to minimize our violence, causing as little harm as possible.

### Food as Ambassador of Ecological Destruction

The fourth contemplation encourages us to keep our compassion alive by reducing suffering to not only living beings, but also to our beautiful mother Earth. If we look deeply at any animal products in our meal, in addition to the suffering of the animals, we will also see that animal agriculture is one of the largest emitters of greenhouse gasses and contributors to global ecosystem devastation.

Animal agriculture wastes enormous quantities of fresh water. It takes 2,500 gallons of water to produce one pound of beef. It takes about a thousand gallons of water to produce one gallon of milk. Animal agriculture is also the leading cause of species extinction, ocean dead zones, water pollution, and habitat destruction. Animal agriculture is the leading cause of global deforestation.

Looking again at Thich Nhat Hanh's "Blue Cliff Letter," we read:

> Buddhist practitioners have practiced vegetarianism over the last 2000 years. We are vegetarian with the intention to nourish our compassion towards the animals. Now we also know that we eat vegetarian in order to protect the earth, preventing global warming from causing her serious and irreversible damage.

Thich Nhat Hanh does not command his students to be vegan, rather, he invites us to look deeply into the consequences of our food choices. He believes that when we see the suffering in our food, and have developed compassion for farmed animals, we will naturally stop consuming animal products.

## Waking Up with Each Bite

In many ways, we are like sleepwalkers living in a dream. We have created a way of eating that is destroying trillions of living beings each year, the web of life on our planet, and ourselves. As followers of the Buddha, "the awakened one," we are called to wake up.

For me, veganism grows out of this path of awakening. The path has not been linear; it has evolved gradually and organically. I have seen new ways to grow my compassion, make changes, and allow those changes to become the new normal. The path of awakening is a path without a destination. It is a path of increasing insight and awareness.

For me, eating is a core practice because it involves looking deeply and cultivating compassion. The Five Contemplations Before Eating guide my eating. I have found that the quality of my eating reflects the quality of my spiritual practice. When my practice is strong, I find myself eating mindfully and looking deeply into each spoonful. When I forget to eat mindfully, it is a sign that my practice is not strong. Because we eat multiple times throughout the day, our meals can be helpful reminders to return to our practice and to our true selves, to look deeply, and in this way weave mindfulness practice into our daily lives. Every bite of food can be an opportunity to practice awareness and compassion. Every bite of food can be an opportunity to awaken.

# Where the Dharma and Animals Meet

BOB ISAACSON

I often wonder what it was that connected me with the suffering of animals. Was it something in my childhood?

I was born and raised in Chicago, and have been an author -ized lay Buddhist teacher for the past dozen years in the Theravadin/Vipassana tradition, having practiced on extensive residential retreats for many years. I am also a vegan animal rights activist and in 2011 co-founded Dharma Voices for Animals (DVA), the only international Buddhist Animal Rights/Advocacy organization.

For twenty-five years, I worked as a human rights/civil rights attorney fighting for the lives of women and men facing the death penalty, primarily in Chicago and San Diego, which included supervising over 500 death penalty cases in the Chicago area as the Death Penalty Coordinator in the Cook County Public Defender's Office. I retired from a satisfying and effective career so I could fully immerse myself in the practice of Buddhism. Not too long after I left Chicago, the Illinois death penalty was abolished, directly saving the lives of nearly 200 women and men.

After making the connection between the animals slaughtered and the food on my plate , I became vegetarian over 40 years ago. I didn't know a single vegetarian and had never heard the word "vegan." In 2004, I became vegan.

What was it then that opened my eyes to the suffering of animals? I loved my dog Wizz who was my best friend during the early part of my life and was always there when I needed him. I remember when I was a young child visiting the Museum of Science and Industry on Chicago's south side. I would always stop at an exhibit that was a live demonstration of baby chicks hatching. The chicks were adorable when they first appeared after pecking their way out of their shells, and experiencing their first taste of life. I fell in love with the chicks and was happy that it appeared they were safe inside this incubator. It never occurred to me that anyone would harm such cute, defenseless animals. I eventually realized that in the real world, billions of baby chicks are hatched each year, and that millions of male chicks are intentionally ground up or suffocated to death in garbage bags, which was probably the fate of the tiny ones I watched being born into life. The challenge for me became to find a way to bring this heartfelt experience of the beauty of the beginning of life and the contrasting experience of unfathomable violence and suffering to the consciousness of Buddhists, and to make it relevant to our Buddhist practice.

An important Dharma teaching is the principle of karma, that we reap what we sow. It is said that someone is eventually reborn into this world with similar habits of mind as in their previous life. It's also said that we should treat all beings with love and compassion because our deceased and prior mothers and fathers might be currently incarnated in another living being. Why then would we harm others?

When I first discovered the Buddha's teachings in 1994, I was deeply touched by his admonition to refrain from harming others, and to treat all beings who can feel pain with compassion. This seemed like a religion and spiritual path with the practice of not eating animals at its core. So, for a number of years I assumed that all the teachers and students were at least vegetarian, if not vegan. It came as a total shock on a cool November day in 2000, several days after the infamous Gore-Bush election, when I walked into our local food market with one of the better-known Western Dharma teachers to buy lunch for the afternoon. We both walked over to the pre-packaged salads with me picking up one with grilled veggies and my companion claiming one with grilled chicken flesh. I quickly attempted to correct his misstep by warning that his selection contained chicken to which he replied with the two words that still haunt me, "I know." I saw my life flash in front of me the next few moments, but more importantly, the mission for the rest of my life had just been born.

The central teaching in the tradition I practice, called Theravada, is to show up in the present moment as much as possible. This practice, called mindfulness, is complemented by a parallel practice called the Brahma Viharas, i.e., heavenly abodes, of which there are four: lovingkindness, compassion, sympathetic joy, and equanimity. The point here is to incline the mind and heart toward each of the four in an organized, disciplined way. The first Brahma Vihara is lovingkindness or *metta* (the word in Pali, the language the Buddha spoke), best understood as friendliness. The instruction, which is quite precise, is to send heartfelt thoughts of kindness to all beings in the universe, animals as well as humans, without distinction. So, it seemed quite certain to me before that November *aha* moment that if we Buddhists continuously send our friendly wishes to fishes, chickens, and pigs, we certainly shouldn't be eating them. But all that changed when I heard, "I know." Certainly, the Buddha could not have instructed his followers to express their unbounded friendliness and kindness to animals on the one hand and on the other hand looked the other way when these same followers chomped into an animal's body. Something was rotten in the state of Dharma.

As one of the most esteemed Buddhist monastics in the world, Dharma Voices for Animals' Advisory Council member Jetsunma Tenzin Palmo, puts it, quoting George Bernard Shaw, "Animals are my friends, and I don't eat my friends." Who would disagree? Or so I thought as I immersed myself in the Buddhist practice by attending one retreat after another.

I soon realized that my life's work was to bring to the attention of Buddhist leaders and centers, starting in the U.S., the disconnect between these sacred teachings on the one hand and, the practice of indifference to our intentional complicity with the terrible suffering we cause animals when we eat them and use the products of their bodies on the other.

Several friends, similarly dismayed and disconnected, did what I did for a number of years after my eye-opening experience in 2000: discuss this disconnect with Buddhist leaders in the West. But, without the power of an organization, no one took us seriously. That all changed when David, Patti, Kim, and I launched Dharma Voices for Animals in 2011. DVA brings like-minded Buddhists together with a single purpose and mission: to be an effective voice for animals in Buddhist countries and communities around the world. As our numbers have grown, so has the strength of our collective voices. Many of the most respected Buddhists in the world have become DVA members and have self-identified as vegan or vegetarian, and Buddhist centers around the world have begun to respond positively to our message.

The good news is that the Buddha's message couldn't be any more animal-friendly, but the bad news is that many, if not most, Buddhists haven't been paying attention. The Dharma teaches us to treat animals as we would other human beings—with kindness, compassion, and without harming them—yet hundreds of millions of Buddhists (of the approximately one billion worldwide) are eating animals and animal products. This non-compliance exacts a significant price from those violating both the spirit and letter of the Buddha's teachings, such as diminished health, an increased sense of disconnectedness and entitlement, and a more challenging meditation practice. Meditation is central to Dharma practice, and the challenge results from living at odds with the Buddha's message of respect for others. But the animals pay a far steeper price for this noncompliance with the Buddha's teachings. They lose their purpose, their freedom, and their very lives.

Being a practicing Buddhist organization, DVA naturally works to encourage Buddhist governments, centers, communities, and individuals to adopt vegan ways of living and practicing. Establishing relationships around the world, DVA as a Buddhist organization can transcend the distrust and suspicion often accompanying interactions that cross cultural and racial lines.

DVA provides international support for those who courageously rock the boat of the establishment by publicly self-identifying as vegan or vegetarian, by talking about which of the numerous teachings by the Buddha inform that choice, and by sharing with others the many advantages of a plant-based diet. It warms my heart to see many Buddhist leaders becoming vocal about their conscious diets.

We all know that the influential and well-funded meat, poultry, fish, and dairy industries have been active in their opposition to plant-based and vegetarian organizations throughout the world. These industries use scare tactics and systematic distortions. As a Buddhist organization, DVA emphasizes that, according to the Buddhist precepts, the truth must be told. We remind Buddhists that we are each individually responsible to articulate these truths: 1) that each year animal agriculture causes the unthinkable suffering of hundreds of billions of defenseless and vulnerable animals, 2) that animal agriculture is the single greatest cause of global environmental devastation, and 3) that leaving animals out of our diet significantly enhances our health.

One common question is, "You do so much to help animals, but what about humans? Why don't you work for them?" Many may respond saying, "I do work for humans. I work for social justice. I advocate for peace. I help political candidates who support equitable solutions such as national health care." My history provides me with a clear answer. As mentioned earlier, as a human rights and civil rights attorney for twenty-five years, I specialized in defending people against the death penalty. My work was literally a matter of life or death for my clients. As a white male, I had the privilege of representing clients who did not have enough money to afford their own attorney. As a public defender, I was appointed by the court. Ninety percent of my clients were people of color. It was impossible to miss the racism directed towards my clients, both in court as well as out of court while I spoke to witnesses, conducted other types of investigations, and in the press. However, every night I returned to my nice home, in a nice neighborhood. You might see where I'm going with this. The work I now do, which is the work many others are doing, is literally a matter of life or death for countless millions, often billions, of defenseless, feeling beings. Both my work on behalf of humans and my work on behalf of animals have involved the protection of vulnerable beings: human rights and animal rights, human protection and animal protection.

Throughout the Buddha's teachings, it is clear that not only are Buddhists expected to refrain from harming humans and animals but also are responsible for protecting them. Yet, many Buddhists worldwide not only fail to protect animals, but are directly involved in causing their suffering. How did we get to this point? Why are many Buddhists around the world attached to the view that as long as we don't kill the animal ourselves, we are not responsible for their death or suffering no matter how complicit we are in the process of their death? Just stating this deluded thinking exposes its baselessness.

So, what does DVA do to protect animals and to be their voice when others, either directly or indirectly, try to harm them? We have a number of programs intending to reach out to as many Buddhists as possible. It is estimated that there are approximately one billion Buddhists in the world with over 98 percent living in Asia, which means that the vast majority of animals killed to feed Buddhists live in Asia. Accordingly, most of our resources are dedicated to Asia.

Throughout Asia most Buddhists seem to accept that they "should" not eat animals, but are worried about practical issues such as nutrition, what to cook, where to buy food, and even how to cook vegetarian or plant-based for some of their family when other family members want to eat animal flesh. Our challenge at DVA is to provide answers and effective support to help people make animal-friendly changes.

The largest number of Buddhists, estimated at between 250 and 750 million, live in China. Other countries with many millions of Buddhists include: Vietnam, Sri Lanka, Thailand, Tibet, Taiwan, Malaysia, South Korea, Myanmar, and Japan. DVA has sponsored two major Asian Buddhist Animal Rights Conferences, one in September, 2016, in Seoul and the other in October, 2017, in Colombo. These were the first two conferences of their kind and our plan is to host similar conferences in Asia every year. In the Buddhist country of Bhutan, we have been publicly challenging the government's plan to build slaughterhouses.

We launched our first large-scale project in a specific Buddhist country, DVA's Sri Lanka Project, in 2017. We hope to use the template created for Sri Lanka in other Buddhist countries and in countries with sizeable Buddhist populations. Our Sri Lanka project implements a social media strategy intended to reach millions of people in that country. We also work to move Sri Lankans toward veganism, or at least vegetarianism, by organizing public events including talks, seminars, workshops, and forums, and using our army of advocates including monastics, political leaders, scientists, nutritionists, and entertainers. In Sri Lanka, we have also been championing landmark animal rights legislation for the past several years.

We have also established and developed chapters in other Asian countries as well as in major population centers in the West. These chapters allow us to have a feel for how Buddhist communities treat animals and what our response should be.

A number of our programs, however, focus on Buddhists in the Western world. For example, *Eyes and Ears* focuses on Buddhist monasteries, temples, and retreat centers, primarily in the West, where we encourage animal-friendly changes that affect the greatest number of animals by limiting the number eaten and setting a positive example for visitors to see. One of the dramatic successes of this program has been at a large Buddhist Center where we successfully ended the practice of serving animal flesh at teacher training retreats and also encouraged reducing, by tens of thousands, the number of eggs used each year.

Our leaders and members give public talks about how the Buddha's teachings should lead us to refrain from eating animals and their products such as eggs, cheese, milk, and butter. I have given public talks around the world, including most of the major U.S. cities as well as many of the largest in Asia and Europe. It's heartening to see that in just over six years Dharma Voices for Animals has become a highly effective global Buddhist animal rights and advocacy group, recognized as a Regional Center by the World Fellowship of Buddhists.

To move Buddhists toward a compassionate diet and to encourage discussion within Buddhist cultures and centers, DVA created a documentary film with Keegan Kuhn that features respected lay and monastic teachers from diverse Buddhist cultures. Appearing in the film, for example, are DVA members Jetsuma Tenzin Palmo, Bhante Gunaratana, the Venerable Geshe Phelgye, Guy and Sally Armstrong, and vegan author Will Tuttle. The film also prominently features Theravadin scholar Bhikku Bodhi, and *A Plea for the Animals* author, the Venerable Matthieu Ricard. Translated now into ten languages, it uses the words of these and other teachers to show the depth and consistency of the Buddha's pro-animal message and to debunk the most commonly used excuses by Buddhists to justify eating animal foods and using the products of their bodies. DVA has also produced a number of materials discussing why Buddhists should stop eating animals. These resources can be found on the *Resources and Right Eating* pages of our website.

Dharma Voices for Animals has close relationships with influential monastics including Master Hai Tao of Taiwan, one of the world's leading animal rights voices, who advocates for compassionate food choices and oversees forty animal sanctuaries in Asia, as well as the Venerable Thich Thanh Huan of Vietnam, a leader in the Vietnamese Buddhist Sangha (VBS), which has tens of millions of followers. We cooperate with these Buddhist leaders to bring DVA's message of compassion for animals to as many Buddhists as possible. Our members receive our e-newsletter that keeps them up to date on what we are doing and are eligible for free plant-based mentoring. Anyone can become a member and support our work on our website.

Dharma Voices for Animals encourages Buddhists, and those open to the message of the Buddha, to talk about and reflect on how animals go from living beings to the food on our plates. This reflection and understanding has led countless Buddhists to turn away from eating animals to far more healthy, sustainable, and respectful plant-based ways of living.

# One Man's Commitment to a Revolution of the Spirit

ARIEL NESSEL

Over three decades ago, at age twelve, I was walking on the Venice Beach Boardwalk while on vacation with my family. A man had set up a booth of sorts along the boardwalk showing in graphic detail how "food animals" are caged and confined, separated from their families, physically abused and eventually slaughtered. I carefully read most of the literature at his table. About thirty minutes later, I went on with my carefree vacation and my merry life, seemingly unaffected.

Fast forward to eleven years later. I'm now 23 and living in California, walking down that same stretch of beach. Looking about a hundred feet ahead, in the same location, I see the same guy in the same booth! I didn't need to approach the booth because in that moment, everything I saw a decade earlier suddenly hit me.

I realized that, by the choices I was currently making, I was perpetuating the horrors I had read about with such great interest as a pre-teen. There was a choice I could make in that moment. I could continue with my current ways, eyes now wide open to the consequences – or – I could stop contributing to these horrors and the suffering endured by animals. It didn't really feel like a choice, though, but more like the universe had finally made me receptive to acknowledging the laws of cause and effect.

At first the insight was mainly about my food choices. I immediately stopped eating land animals and, over the next five years, gradually eliminated the secretions of land animals and the bodies of sea animals from my diet. I found as I began to further pull on the threads of this unjust and wicked system, it became hard to ignore how interconnected food is with culture, and culture is with ignorance, and ignorance is with *dukkha* (suffering).

That day was the beginning of a new awareness. By some great fortune, I was able to recognize the connection between cause and effect and I started to appreciate how every choice I made had an impact. It was the realization that my choices always matter, and in whatever I do, there will be always ripples.

The experience of that fateful day led me on a long journey that continues today. The journey is an inquiry into my interconnection with all of life, and a longing to use the precious time I have in this human body to embody qualities I now know as wisdom and compassion.

This new path I was on, which some might call a path of *ahimsa*, was pulling me to question my unexamined assumptions about what constitutes success in life. If three times each day I was unwittingly contributing to some of the worst abuses imaginable, what else was I involved with that was also antithetical to my deeply-held values? Where else was I sleepwalking through life? If something so blatantly obvious had been imperceptible to me, what would it take for me to adjust my awareness so that the familiar could be seen with new eyes? What would it take to have vision less conditioned and blinded by culture, upbringing, and selfishness?

As I tried to answer these questions, the insights from that day on the boardwalk became more embodied and integral to my being. It became clear to me that getting what I wanted was not going to actually get me what I really wanted – happiness. I could see myself two decades hence, at the pinnacle of worldly success and achieving the American dream, yet still wondering "is this all there really is?"

Not knowing what options and alternatives existed, I began my own spiritual quest. Up to that point I was highly atheistic and skeptical of organized religion, which I saw as its own form of delusion. I had always been a bit rebellious (which worked well in my transition to becoming vegan). This, combined with a chip on my shoulder, disinclined me from traditions that demanded a form of faith that trusted the insights and experiences of others. Also, if any spiritual practice was worth its salt, it would have a strong moral framework that honored the lives of more than one-one millionth of the species on this planet.

After reading books about various prophets, gurus, spiritual practices and religions, however, I felt no closer to an answer. Most of the people I read about were dead and their teachings were not accessible to me except through books. However, one day in 1998 I somehow came across a Zen Buddhist temple in Hamtramck, Michigan (I had recently moved back to Michigan earlier that year). I read a bit about a guy named Buddha and went to check the Buddhists out.

Early on a cold winter Sunday, my girlfriend and I went to visit their weekly public gathering. When we got there, we followed everyone else and proceeded to sit on a round pillow on the floor. Then suddenly a bell was rung, and everyone went completely quiet. It all seemed strange. I looked around the room for what seemed like an eternity, seeing all these people just doing nothing. Always used to doing something, I felt a heightened sense of discomfort. The bizarreness was amplified by several folks there with shaved heads dressed in grey robes. Then, abruptly, the guy at the front rang the bell again. Now everyone began chanting unfamiliar words, mostly in an unfamiliar language, in a weird cadence, in a most unmelodious way. Finally, they stopped. The fellow at the front then proceeded to give what I now know to be a dharma talk.

None of this had much of an impact on me. However, after it was all done, I took one long last look around the room as we departed. I saw a certain lightness in these people. Their faces somehow seemed softer, their smiles brighter, their demeanor more at ease. I distinctly remember saying to my girlfriend, "I don't know what those people were doing in there. However, if doing it gets them that sort of result, then I am willing to try it." Twenty years later, I am still trying it!

For many people, a deepening Buddhist practice leads to a gradual expansion of their moral circle. Eventually that leads to the inclusion of the animals they mostly know as breakfast, lunch and dinner, until one day they are unable to eat beings they now recognize to be sentient and worthy of kindness. For me, it worked in the opposite order. The suffering of others, and my longing to reduce their suffering, led me on my spiritual journey. However, either one without the other would be insufficient.

Over the years I have attempted to integrate the wing of compassion with the wing of wisdom to create a revolution within my own heart. At first it seemed more like the two were completely separate endeavors. I would meditate daily and go on silent retreats multiple times each year. Simultaneously, I dutifully advocated for farm animals, passing out leaflets about the horrors of animal agriculture and participating in various protests (even donning costumes when helpful). I also began a personal practice of "earn to give," seeking to use my skills in the business world to provide financial resources to the farm animal advocacy movement. In time, I saw the transformative power of compassionate action, not just for those being harmed and society at large, but for me, the activist. Wanting to support, empower and encourage a movement away from apathy and towards engagement, I co-founded The Pollination Project.

Over time, however, I felt like I was bifurcating my essential nature into two distinct people, Ari the activist and Ari the spiritual practitioner. This approach was oddly amplified by the sanghas I had been exposed to. The dharma teachers openly condoned eating animals and were also disinclined towards seeing activism as a potentially skillful manifestation of compassion.

I wanted to live out my full 'Ari-ness" and could not find a place where this was embraced. Activist circles were highly focused on impact. Buddhist circles were focused on intention.

Through my longing for greater wholeness, I am now on a path to reconcile the two, seeing how tightly intertwined the dharma is with social justice, and how integrated my liberation is with the freedom of all sentient beings. To that end, I have begun to host meditation retreats and workshops for activists and encourage fellow Buddhists to, as Thich Nhat Hanh has said, make compassion a verb. I've also helped co-create a retreat center called Banyan Grove, in my role as a volunteer with Service Space, as a place to support this integrated ethic.

It is remarkable how much impact one person can have on the world. I knew that the man at Venice Beach, who I now know as Jingles, might never know that his choice to show up on that boardwalk and educate people about animal suffering would change the course of my life. And yet, his commitment to ending animal suffering led him to set up a booth and dedicate his life to it for twenty-five years, without acknowledgement, praise or recognition.

Jingles is a constant reminder to me that we never really know who we have influenced. We influence people by everything we do, from what we wear, to the bike we ride, to the job we have, to the car we drive, to the food we eat, to the products we buy, to the time we spend in silence, to the time we spend in activity, and by all of our thoughts, words, and deeds. It all has an impact.

Buddhism has taught me that unless I pay close attention to my six senses, I will ride the endless, discontented roller coaster of seeking pleasure and avoiding pain. Most likely, in the process, I will limit my ability to create the change I seek in the world. Without awareness and internal transformation, I will be planting lemon seeds and hoping they sprout oranges.

My friend Pancho Ramos-Stierle sums it well: "It is time for the spiritual people to get active and the activist people to get spiritual so that we can have a total revolution of the human spirit."

# Are Vipassana and Veganism Compatible?

WILLIAM DIGIORGIO

~~~~~~~~~~~~~~~~~~~~~~~~~~~~~~~~~~~~~~~~~~~~~~~~~~~~~~~~~~~~~~~~~~~~~~

Eight years ago, I began my Buddhist Vipassana practice by attending my first ten-day meditation course. How unlikely it was for me, someone who had been diagnosed with Attention Deficit Disorder, to sit still—let alone try to focus my mind in meditation—for hours at a time! Yet, the feeling of liberation and tranquility at the conclusion of those ten days shifted the path of my life.

I didn't maintain my Vipassana practice with perfect consistency from day one, just as I didn't maintain veganism (a practice I had adopted a few years earlier) with perfect consistency. However, over time, by attending a number of courses and with regular practice at home, I experienced many benefits including greater patience, reduced anger, and a more balanced mind. I believe it has also made me a kinder person, helping me to recognize everyone as my brother and sister, just as I recognize animals as my equals.

Besides the difficulty of making time for a ten-day meditation course, one of the biggest concerns for first-time students is what kind of food they will be served. As most are omnivores, they may worry about whether they will be satisfied with the vegetarian menu. In contrast, my concern as a vegan was whether I would find food that was animal-free, so I was relieved to find most everything served was vegan. While there are dairy products—such as milk, cheese, yogurt, and butter—they are usually on the side, and optional.

During my raw vegan phase, I was concerned about whether there would be enough raw fruits and vegetables to subsist (the answer is: probably not, but it depends on the meditation center, of which there are dozens around the world). However, as I attended more meditation courses, the food seemed to matter less.

## For Whom the Bell Tolls: Old Students vs. New Students

Every day at eleven a.m., a bell is rung for lunch. During the first one or two courses, I often became distracted and impatient toward the end of the morning meditation session, and would be anxiously awaiting the bell. At times I could have sworn I heard it chiming, but it was just my imagination. To be sure not to miss the bell, I got in the habit of frequently checking the time and drifting out of the meditation hall toward the dining hall. Often I was at the head of the line, or not far back. I always ate too much and became drowsy in the afternoon, despite the teachers' warnings against over-eating. I discovered that meditation requires more energy than one might think.

At five p.m., the bell is rung again to announce dinner time. While the new students are served fruit and tea, "old students" (those who are have completed at least one course) can only drink tea. It was annoying at first to watch the new students savoring the fruit, but eventually I got used to it. I realized that it is part of the practice to overcome adversity, and to free ourselves from attachments in order to become equanimous and pure.

Becoming vegan had meant giving up strong attachments to foods I had been eating for over four decades. In my Italian-American upbringing, every holiday revolved around eating animal products. Then, as an adult with a stressful lifestyle, I had become even more attached to animal flesh, cheeses and alcohol. I lived for them, and many of my friendships and work relationships were forged around them. Giving up these substances sometimes meant giving up relationships, too. It would not be an exaggeration to say that even my mother wanted to disown me for not eating her meatballs and her eggplant parmigiana.

Fast forward several years, to the meditation center. I consider it a mark of progress that I am calmer and no longer among the first ones lined up to eat lunch. I am still working on not overeating, but it's not easy because the food is tasty and filled with the loving kindness of the volunteer cooks. After growing accustomed to not eating anything from noon until six a.m. the following morning (fasting for eighteen hours a day), I have also experimented with keeping up this schedule at home for some period of time after returning from the course.

## Dhamma Service (Volunteering)

As an old student, in addition to maintaining a daily meditation practice, we are encouraged to volunteer to serve at courses to develop our *parami* (Buddha-like qualities).

As Dhamma servers, not only are we helping those who come to sit the course to stay focused on their meditation, but also we have an opportunity to assimilate our meditation practice into our work while interacting with others (servers are allowed to speak when necessary to perform their jobs, whereas students must observe "noble silence" throughout the course).

Servers perform administrative responsibilities or kitchen jobs. I have served courses a number of times and, as an avid home cook, working in the Vipassana center's kitchen (equipped with a huge commercial stove) for the first time gave me quite a thrill. In fact, cooking for Vipassana courses inspired me to change careers and pursue becoming a vegan chef as a profession.

Unfortunately, as time has gone on, I have begun to feel a growing unease while serving courses because the breakfast, lunch and evening snacks we put together are accompanied by dairy products (and let's leave aside the question of honey, which is also present).

**Vegan's Dilemma**

While it didn't used to bother me as a student, now as a server I am required to offer dairy products to others. This feels as though I am condoning these options and therefore complicit in the abuse that cows have had to endure. And so I began to discuss my feelings with others in the organization.

First, I asked a long-term kitchen volunteer why the meals were not completely vegan. She said it was to make students feel comfortable, and that it was not our place to force a particular diet upon anybody. I inquired of the teacher assistants about it during the time set aside for consultation. They reiterated the same explanation, and also tried to steer the conversation back to the meditation technique. To them, the type of food served was just another distraction that I needed to overcome. But was it really?

According to the Vipassana Code of Discipline that all those attending a course agree to follow, the foundation of the practice is *sila* — moral conduct. Sila provides a basis for the development of *samadhi*, concentration of mind, and purification of the mind is achieved through *pañña*, the wisdom of insight.

Everyone also agrees to follow the five Buddhist precepts for the duration of a course, and ideally carry them into daily life. We are to abstain from killing any being, to abstain from stealing, to abstain from sexual activity, to abstain from telling lies, and to abstain from intoxicants.

Founding teacher S.N. Goenka (who passed away in 2013, but still teaches the course via pre-recorded videos) mentions the subject of killing animals in one of his evening discourses and the topic is further explored in *The Art of Living*, a well-known book by William Hart who has been teaching Vipassana since 1982.

In a chapter entitled "The Training of Moral Conduct," the Buddha paraphrases the Noble Eightfold Path to eradicate suffering as follows: "Abstain from all unwholesome deeds, perform wholesome ones, purify your mind—this is the teaching of all enlightened persons."

On the topic of "Right Livelihood," the book states the two criteria of Right Livelihood.

> First it should not be necessary to break the five precepts in one's work, since doing so obviously causes harm to others. But further, one should not do anything that encourages other people to break the precepts, since this will also cause harm. Neither directly nor indirectly should our means of livelihood involve injury to other beings. Thus any livelihood that involves killing, whether of human beings or of animals, is clearly not right livelihood. But even if the killing is done by others and one simply deals in the parts of slaughtered animals, their skins, flesh, bones, and so on, still this is not right livelihood, because one is depending on the wrong actions of others.

Further, the author posed the following questions to Goenka.

Q: Is it breaking sila to eat meat?

A: No, not unless you have killed the animal your-self. If meat happens to be provided for you and you enjoy its taste as you would that of any other food, you have not broken any precept. But of course, by eating meat, you indirectly encourage someone else to break the precepts by killing. And also at subtler level, you harm yourself by eating meat. Every moment an animal generates craving and aversion; it is incapable of observing itself, of purifying its mind. Every fiber of its body becomes permeated with craving and aversion. This is the input you receive when eating non-vegetarian food. A meditator is trying to eradicate craving and aversion, and therefore would find it helpful to avoid such food.

Q: It that why vegetarian food is served at a course?

A: Yes, because it is best for Vipassana meditation.

Q: Do you recommend vegetarianism in daily life?

A: That is also helpful.[1]

I have the utmost respect and gratitude for Goenka's selfless dedication to spreading this valuable technique for eradicating suffering, and I also have no doubt he was intelligent. Assuming he was aware of the animal cruelty inflicted in dairy production, wouldn't he have felt that abstaining from dairy products would develop stronger sila?

Having written about my Vipassana experiences on my blog, I have received many comments from fellow vegan students and prospective students who feel conflicted about being part of a practice that does not demonstrate compassion for all animals, thereby somehow diminishing their vegan sila or morality. While acknowledging the disconnect, I have defended the organization's position and praised the technique, which has helped thousands, and have encouraged others to concentrate on their practice and look on the bright side. Most people attending the courses are being exposed to a vegetarian diet for the first time, which is a step in the right direction. Nonetheless, I have felt that we should continue to communicate our concerns to the leadership.

## Hope and Dialog

With Goenka's passing in 2013, hundreds of his assistant teachers became teachers in their own right, and I hoped they might be able to reform food policy, even if only by veganizing one region or center at a time. However, a teacher informed me that the decisions are still made in India, and that it's unlikely people in India would ever agree to abstain from dairy products.

Never one to give up, I had been e-mailing my inquiry to the Dhamma organization headquarters in India for months before recently receiving the below reply:

Perhaps you are aware that half a century ago S.N. Goenka began teaching Vipassana in India, and the meditation spread from there around the world. To this day, however, by far the most Vipassana centers and meditators are located in India. All the centers follow a common set of rules. One of these is to serve simple, vegetarian food. In India that is defined as serving no food containing meat, fish, fowl or eggs. Milk and milk products are not excluded, however. And in fact, in India — which has tens or hundreds of millions of lifelong vegetarians — milk has always been regarded as a perfect food and cows are traditionally treated with reverence. The diet served at centers there is the diet that all Indians of any background can accept. When centers were founded in other countries, they adopted the same rules that S.N. Goenka had put in place for centers in India. Over the years, especially in Western countries, centers have reduced their reliance on milk and milk products, reflecting a gradual change in eating habits; for example, centers usually do not use milk or cheese when cooking, or else they offer a non-dairy alternative. But they still have milk and milk products available for those who wish to add them, for example, to a hot drink or to a bowl of cereal. It is each individual student's choice whether to consume dairy or only vegan food. It is not our mission to promote any particular diet. What we do provide is strictly in line with the Five Precepts for moral conduct set out by the Buddha. It is what places for Vipassana meditation have done for many centuries. If at some time the overwhelming majority of people in a country become vegan, centers would probably choose to provide a strictly vegan diet for all. But we are far away from that situation today. Until then, centers will continue providing vegetarian food that is acceptable to the general population.

With best wishes, M.M. Khandhar, Teacher.

While I was disappointed with the content of the reply, I was grateful to finally be acknowledged and to have begun a dialog. As I began to consider drafting my response, another email message arrived. This message was from William Hart himself. It said: "It is quite likely that the person will seek to start an ongoing debate. If he replies to this message, I recommend not answering. Metta, Bill"

I felt deeply discouraged by this second message, which was obviously not intended for me. I started to lose my equanimity, and wondered how I could continue to follow this path when the leaders clung to their traditions without considering their consequences. As long as they are not vegans themselves, why would they even consider changing the policy?

At this point, I recalled the meditation we practice for a few minutes at the end of each session, called *Metta Bhavana* or Loving Kindness: "May all beings be peaceful, be happy, be liberated. May all beings share my peace, my harmony, my merits."

With Will Tuttle's permission, and with much Metta, I would like to publish my open response to M. Khandhar here:

> Thank you for your response. I understand you want to maintain the traditions of the past. After all, the meditation technique and the course materials have stood the test of time and benefitted countless people, myself included. However, much has changed in animal agriculture since the days of the Buddha and dramatically so in the past fifty years. A recent documentary explained that because cows cannot be slaughtered in some states in India, they are being abusively transported to other states for slaughter once they have outlived their profitability to their owners. Would you not agree that a vegan diet greatly reduces animal suffering and killing? Shouldn't we be striving for the highest morality before we attempt to purify ourselves through meditation? Rather than waiting for the habits of the general population to change, couldn't you endorse abstaining from dairy products, at least during the course? Can we try adopting a fully vegan menu somewhere in the United States? I would be honored if there is any way I can help with this

initiative that will begin to bring about a great healing in the world. At least, I would appreciate the opportunity for a continued dialog with you on this important matter.

References:
1.      William Hart, The Art of Living. Harper One, 1987, page 66.

# What is Negativity?

JOHN BUSSINEAU

My late teacher of twenty years, Kyabje Gelek Rimpoche, described the essence of negativity in simple terms, "Negativity is the harming of sentient beings, including yourself."[1] If harming others is negative, what is positive? Helping others, according to Rimpoche.

Who are other sentient beings? Buddhism has a universal outlook that includes humans, animals and insects. As such, the Buddha spoke of *sabbe sattva*, or all beings, in the Pali Canon, from the first teachings. Other beings deserve our active compassion because they are not different from humans other than in form. We understand that life is dear to all beings, and in this way, we are the same. For this reason, it is a Buddhist's responsibility to help rather than harm others.

How we learn to help ourselves and other beings, by doing less harm, is central to Buddhist practice and is a foundational consideration in every teaching tradition. Meditation is emphasized, as well as cultivating an ongoing practice of analysis of our personal involvements, including our most basic actions, behaviors, and customs. This is the ethical foundation for our spiritual path. It is where we mindfully examine our behavior and attitudes, and is embodied in the first precept: do not kill; do not be an accessory to killing; do not destroy life; practice non-violence; respect life. This precept seems to be central to virtually all spiritual paths. It can be enormously challenging, however, because when we investigate our actions we often find harm toward others or ourselves.

In Buddhism there are no strict rules on ethics because the Buddha pointed toward ethical behavior with teachings on meditation, learning, and most importantly by analyzing causes and conditions. The first precept, and other Buddhist teachings, point toward the moon but are not the moon. As each situation has different causes and conditions, each must be analyzed using our hearts (empathetic and compassionate introspection) along with personal and scientific data. The Buddha wanted us not to follow blindly but to think, analyze, test, and consider the consequences of our actions so that we can learn to reduce the harm we cause. This introspection forms the basis for analytical meditation, a step-by-step cognitive form of *samadhi* (meditation) that leads to greater understanding of our connectedness to all life.

In analyzing my own actions, I found I was breaking preliminary ethical considerations in many areas of my life. We are all works in progress because ego, anger, and negative emotions are challenging to eradicate. It is also difficult to let go of our attachment to material goods and services and the basic structural violence they engender in today's world. The practices of mindfulness and meditation, over twenty years, helped knock some of my shallow egocentric ways down. However, one area was embarrassingly hidden for a long time: my consumption of meat, dairy, and eggs. In 2010, I found myself at a divide in the road, where I needed to make a decision for my health, the environment, and other sentient beings. I came to the realization that I was compromising my ethical values without knowing it and had been doing so for most of my life, including those times when was a vegetarian. My carnivorous habits were creating enormous harm, and I resisted contemplating the first precept for fear of uncovering the uncomfortable truth. Nevertheless, I did probe, and realized that cows, pigs, chickens, fishes, and all the animals we consider food are sentient beings who yearn to live, who suffer at our hands, and who will cling to their lives with the last bit of their strength. My diet was creating negativity for myself and other beings but I didn't want to face this. I was attached to eating animals, and I was not respecting life.

## Harming Ourselves

In early 2010, at age 55, I was on a statin drug to lower cholesterol and triglycerides, as are many Americans are who eat a standard American diet. My total cholesterol hovered around 230 while on medication. My triglycerides were mostly off the charts. I had high blood pressure at every annual physical; however, because it was at the "low end of high" I refused blood pressure medications. My sugar levels were also high each time, being at the top of the normal range year after year which made me pre-diabetic. My BMI, a measure of weight, put me just into the category of obese. I was heading for a heart attack, stroke, diabetes and a bag full of daily medications to counteract my diet. I was harming myself and creating negativity.

When I stopped eating animals something miraculous happened. My cholesterol dropped to 155 and my triglycerides normalized, as did my blood pressure, sugar levels and weight. This change was predicted by most contemporary medical research. We now know, with certainty, that a whole-foods plant-based diet promotes health, and that animal protein in any form tends to promote disease. We have been losing the war on the eradication of heart disease, diabetes, and cancer for years due to our food choices. People love to hear that bacon and eggs are healthy for breakfast, that chicken is better than red meat (even though it is higher in cholesterol), and that fish is good for our omega fatty acid levels. People still flock to dairy products and yogurt to improve health, often craving casein, the main protein in milk and cheese, even though it is has been shown repeatedly to be toxic to humans.[2]

Continuing to eat animals is a result of the ego talking to us. It is our own biases, tastes, and habits telling us it's okay to keep doing what we've been doing. We are attached to doing harm to ourselves and ignoring the harm we cause others. Reality and the data available tell us a sobering story. Obesity is on the rise with one third of all adults categorized as such. In the U.S., heart disease is still the number one killer, with 600,000 deaths per year.[3] Cancer rates are growing and diabetes has become epidemic, all due to eating animal foods.[4]

My lifestyle was certainly creating negativity and was harming me. But was it really hurting other beings too? I didn't kill animals purposely. I didn't tell slaughterhouses to kill cows, chickens, pigs and fishes for me. They were already dead when I purchased them. I didn't tell dairy farms to take newborn calves from their mothers so their milk could be collected. I was following the Buddhist three rules of purity: it wasn't killed for me; I had not seen it killed nor had I heard it killed. These of course are all outdated ideas from 2,500 years ago when monks begged for food on daily alms walks in local villages.

## Harming Other Beings

I realized that the three purity rules are something behind which Buddhists who choose to eat animal foods can hide. Buddhist practitioners can use these rationalizations, even though they do not beg for food or live in the Buddha's time. I needed to understand this and to realize that we live in a time of precise marketing strategies and communication tactics designed to manipulate thoughts, perspectives, and buying patterns. Most purchases in our global economy are analyzed after going into databases, and everything is accounted for. Thus, when I purchased a one-pound package of ground beef to make the family pasta sauce recipe, I was putting in an order for another package of ground beef. I was the cause and condition for another animal to be forcibly impregnated and killed on my behalf. I didn't know the animal, had not seen or heard the animal killed, and knew the animal was not specifically killed for me, but this ancient set of rules is irrelevant in today's world. If we don't purchase animal foods, there will be no jobs for people to kill and dismember animals at slaughterhouses. Without demand there is no supply. Without buyers and consumers of animal foods, there is no killing of animals. We become killers of life when we purchase animal-sourced products through the market system.

I was sitting on my Mahayana cushion of meditation, wishing to free sentient beings from suffering and the causes of suffering, and then ordering them on my plate every day for breakfast, lunch, and dinner. My daily meditation practice utilized core Buddhist intentional phrases, mantra recitation, visualizations, and of course watching the breath and the elusive and jumping mind. Some of the phrases I used were related to generation of loving-kindness:

"In my heart I turn to the Three Jewels of refuge.
May I free suffering beings and place them in bliss.
May the compassionate spirit of love grow within me.

That I may complete the enlightening path."

"By practicing generosity and the other perfections may I be able to obtain enlightenment, for the benefit of all sentient beings."

"May all sentient beings enjoy happiness and the cause of happiness. How wonderful it would be. May this be accomplished. I will bring them happiness and the causes of happiness. Bless me to accomplish this."

"May all sentient beings be free from suffering and the cause of suffering. How wonderful it would be. May this be accomplished. I will free them from suffering and the cause of suffering. Bless me to accomplish this."

The intention of my Buddhist practice was to bring happiness to other beings and alleviate their suffering, but when I looked at the breast of the barbequed chicken on my plate, I didn't see a once-living, breathing creature. I was blind, my feelings were turned off, and I was disconnected from those intentional phrases of my practice.

It was not until I stopped eating animal foods and took the vegan pledge for 30 days that I began to see the truth of what was on my plate – the remains of a life of misery, enslavement, and abuse. Here was a chicken, a once sentient creature who had been raised on a factory farm in horrendous conditions. She had had vital interests, and she had suffered. She had yearned for freedom but had never received it. She would have naturally enjoyed basking in the sunlight and taking dust baths but never had the opportunity. Her natural capacity to converse and be a part of her community of hens and roosters had been frustrated, as were all her natural tendencies. She had endured an unmerciful slaughter, fighting to free herself from the arms grabbing and shoving her into a cage. She had been put on a slaughter shipment truck and ruthlessly pulled from the cage upon arrival, where she struggled as she hung upside down on the slaughter line, wriggling and moving continuously, fighting to avoid the razor sharp blade that cut her precious throat.

Whether it is a glass of milk, an egg, or any animal body-part, when we analyze what is on our plates, we find harm to another being and the creation of negativity. We find disrespect for life. We do not find generosity but its opposite, selfishness, deceit, and fear. This is a form of analytical meditation I should have been doing all the while but was not. I was a miserable dharma practitioner when I was eating meat, fish, dairy, and eggs. I was not living my intentions but ignoring them due to my attachment to my habits and taste buds. Then I learned that on top of causing untold harm to sentient beings, I was causing tremendous negativity to planet Earth as well.

**Harming the Planet**

When we analyze animal agriculture operations, particularly Confined Area Feeding Operations (CAFOs) we find one of the most destructive and wasteful industries on the planet. Over ninety-five percent of all land animals we eat today are raised in these hellish environments. Animals, grain, water, and energy, all the inputs of production, are controlled as commodities requiring the massive growing of crops, the birthing and feeding of billions of animals, their slaughter and dismemberment, refrigeration and shipping, and sales and marketing. Beings are reduced to things with cold and ironic efficiency in this most wasteful of industries. The goal of the CAFOs that produce our meat, dairy, and eggs is to maximize speed, and fatten and exploit the animals as cheaply as possible. Every burger we buy and every piece of cheese we eat is a vote for this system of destruction.

Eating animals is responsible for creating dead zones in the world's oceans due to massive farm fertilizer runoff that is generated by the feed crops for the seventy billion land animals we slaughter annually. In fact, almost half of the earth's land mass is devoted to growing livestock feed and grazing animals. In 2006, in an attempt to formulate climate change culpability, the United Nations released a report that stated that animal agriculture is accountable for eighteen percent of greenhouse gas emissions, more than all transportation combined.[5] The eighteen percent figure we now know is an underestimate, with the 2009 WorldWatch study putting the figure at fifty-one percent of our human greenhouse gas footprint.[6]

And while climate change gets all the attention because we can measure, see, and feel it, global depletion is just as tragic if not worse. We are depleting our water, land, rainforests, and wildlife animal populations in an unprecedented manner due to the inherent wastefulness of animal agriculture.[7] We are depleting and polluting fresh water, which should and could be a renewable resource, but is not, because we use it in such vast amounts.[8] We are draining forty major global aquifers faster than their recharge rates.[9] We are burning off the lungs of the planet by destroying rainforests at a rate of one to two acres every second.[10] Due to rainforest destruction alone, it is estimated that 130 plant, animal, and insect species become extinct daily. Coral reef life is all but vanishing due to pollution and over-fishing. We humans are causing the sixth great extinction, now named the Anthropocene (caused by humans), by killing off more species in just a few decades than in the last 65 million years. Oceanographers predict that the world's oceans will be wholly devoid of fish by 2048.[11] Bees and other insects are dying, and wildlife clings to narrow marginal areas because native forests, grasslands, and wetlands are disappearing under the relentless pressure of animal agriculture.[12]

The good news is that we can take 25 to 50 percent of greenhouse gas emissions out of the climate change equation collectively by changing our dietary choices. Not a single company needs to change, not one protest needs to happen, or a single governmental ruling. We can each change our mind, our habits, and spread the word. When comparing a standard American diet with a vegan diet, we find that with a single decision we can reduce our personal environmental footprint to the equivalent of one eleventh of the fossil fuels, one thirteenth of the water, and one sixteenth of the land of animal food production.

When I learned this in 2010, I realized that my eating habits were directly connected to the killing of our planet, causing extinction, annihilating wildlife, and killing the oceans. Plus, it was the cause of immense negativity and harm to my health. It became clear to me that I must become a vegan because this completely encapsulates the Buddhist path of respect for life, and causing less harm and negativity.

## Feed Conversion Rates and Plant Sentience

Spiritual practitioners are concerned about all life forms on Earth and thus the question of plant sentience often comes into question when discussing the eating of meat. Vegans often hear, "But plants are sentient too." This is used to argue that something has to die in order for us to live. Yet, many times it is used to justify the continuation of bad habits, deflecting responsibility, and curtailing open dialogue. The argument goes something like this. "Vegetarians and vegans don't realize they also are responsible for killing insects, rodents, and other animals when they choose to eat plants. Plants are sentient too." This is an interesting discussion point, because if we care about the entire Earth including the plants, trees, forests, and oceans, we will eventually realize that plant-based eating minimizes our harm of not just animals but plants as well. This may seem counterintuitive unless we understand feed conversion ratios.

Agricultural corporations and farmers understand how much plant matter is needed to feed cows, chickens, turkeys, and pigs. To create one pound of beef, it takes about sixteen pounds of soybeans and corn (e.g., grain and feed.) To create one pound of bacon it takes seven to eight pounds of grain and feed.[13] Let's

compare this to a family of four eating one meal. If each consumes a quarter-pound beef hamburger, they each just ate the four pounds of beans plus the quarter-pound of animal flesh. Together they consumed the equivalent of sixteen pounds of soybeans and corn in one sitting, plus a pound of flesh. To do less harm, would it not have been a better choice to grow and cook only one pound of beans and give fifteen pounds of beans to others who need the food and save the cow's life? Or to give the fifteen pounds back to the Earth, never to have been grown in the first place? This would allow the farm land go back to forest, restoring needed habitat to help wildlife thrive, including trees, plants, and animals. The point is, when we analyze all the causes and conditions, we find that we kill much less plant life when we choose to eat only plants.

When we decide to eat meat, we are being more harmful on every level, and collectively, we cause untold trillions of plants to die.[14] Biologists estimate that a vegan saves at least a hundred trees annually.[15] The amount of grain we feed to animals each year in the United States alone could feed 800 million people—if we didn't feed it to animals.[16] Essentially we have the ability to end global hunger by simply transitioning from eating animals to plants.

**Nargarjuna and the Case for Pure Vegetarianism**
Nargarjuna, the famous Buddhist monk who is held in high esteem for his illuminating treatises on the middle path, is quoted as saying, *shunyata karuna garbham*, which literally means, "emptiness is the birthplace of compassion."[17] Rather than voidness or emptiness, I prefer to use the doorstep concept of dependent origination. Dependent origination is the understanding of relativity; everything is interrelated, connected, and relative. Direct experience and knowledge of dependent origination comes to us when we realize that everything we do is linked in some way, shape, or form to all other beings and events. All things

dependently arise in the web of birth, death, and becoming. We are all joined; what I do affects you and what you do affects me. The Buddha used very simple terms to describe this – when this is present, that arises, and when this is absent, that does not arise.

When we realize this and understand the concept of dependent origination and causality, we find compassion for others overwhelms us and we wish to find ways to help those others. It is a boomerang effect, a fundamental Buddhist teaching. We realize that hurting other beings is just like hurting ourselves. When we see the connection between all living beings with open hearts, and when we realize we are indeed empty of a fundamentally separate self, *Mahakaruna*, great compassion, arises within us. Helping other beings, alleviating their suffering, and working to free them from bondage brings happiness, love, and more compassion. When we realize this, we can no longer eat animals because this causes them to be imprisoned and killed for us. When we stop harming others by not eating them, we help them and we feel better. This is an engagement of the heart.

For example, some Buddhist teachers have verbalized that dairy cows are practicing the paramita of generosity in giving their baby's milk to us. The reality, however, is that dairy cows yearn to be free and have their offspring near them. They do not want their milk and calves stolen from them, or to live in barren concrete encampments with a life span of only four to five years before being sent off to slaughter, rather than their twenty-five year normal lifespan. Dairy cows, like all other sentient beings, are here with us, not for us.

The same is true for chickens who lay eggs, pigs who have piglets, and all sentient life forms including wildlife whose habitat is destroyed with every acre we burn to grow more crops for animal food. When we understand our relationship to other sentient beings, we realize that refraining from eating them eliminates the market conditions for their incarceration and death. Thus, not eating them expresses and engenders compassion.

I went through my life thinking I was a moral and compassionate person. I worked, paid my bills, took care of my family, and tried to learn as much about Buddhist practice as I could. Then, I implemented this practice in my life, trying to be good to all humans, fair and open. It wasn't until I stopped eating beings and their secretions that the profound realization occurred that I had been living a lie. I was contributing to the structural violence that relentlessly enslaves, rapes, and slaughters billions of animals every year, and realized I had been blinded by my upbringing, culture, and personal tastes, and that my inner values did not match my outer actions. It was the Buddhist practice of awakening.

## The Four Noble Truths From Vegan Eyes

Following the Buddha's teaching on the Four Noble Truths helps us to change our habits. These four truths are broken into two sets: two negative truths (the truth of suffering and of the cause of suffering) and two positive truths (that there is a way out, and the path to do so). To become an ethical vegan, we simply follow the Buddha's instructions by looking at the Four Noble Truths through the eyes of animals. First, we find the truth of suffering and nowhere is this more evident than in the billions of animals we raise only to kill. They die, we die, wildlife and hungry people die, and the planet dies. This is the truth of suffering; this is negativity.

The second truth informs us of the cause of suffering, that is, our own ignorance, due to our conditioned response to like some, dislike others, and become indifferent to many. This is sometimes explained as attachment and aversion. We are indifferent to animals' lives and their suffering because we are attached to their flesh, milk, and eggs. This is ignorance.

The third truth informs us that there is a way out of this suffering. We can be free of eating animal foods and live a vegan lifestyle. The fourth truth is the actual path to freedom that is built on the awareness that we have the capability to be mindful in the face suffering and to choose to be an ethical vegan. This is the path to becoming a fully awakened Buddha. Taking a 30-day vegan pledge as a path to becoming more ethical can help us transform and renew our mind. As we stop eating animal foods, more compassion arises and a sense of connectedness can be born in us. This is what is needed in today's world—a greater sense of connectedness—and when we connect to all, we can bring about both inner harmony and world peace.

**References:**
1. Remembering Gelek Rimpoche, Lions Roar: https://www.lionsroar.com/remebering-gelek-rimpoche-tibetan-buddhist-teacher-and-author-1939-2017/
2. T. Colin Campbell, "Casein Consumption," February, 2010. http://nutritionstudies.org/casein-consumption/
3. "Heart Disease Facts," Centers for Disease Control, Underlying Cause of Death 1999-2013 on CDC WONDER Online Database, released 2015. https://www.cdc.gov/heartdisease/facts.htm
4. See, for example, these documentary films: *Forks Over Knives; Eating You Alive; Food Choices;* and *What the Health.*
5. "Livestock a major threat to environment," FAO Newsroom, United Nations Food and Agriculture Organization, November 2006. http://www.fao.org/Newsroom/en/news/2006/1000448/index.html
6. Robert Goodland and Jeff Anhang, "Livestock and Climate Change," Worldwatch Institute. December 2009. http://www.worldwatch.org/node/6294
7. Richard Oppenlander, "Freshwater Abuse and Loss: Where is it All Going?" May 2013. https://www.forksoverknives.com/freshwater-abuse-and-loss-where-is-it-all-going/
8. "Irrigation and Water Use," U.S. Department of Agriculture, April 2018. https://www.ers.usda.gov/topics/farm-practices-management/irrigation-water-use/
9. "The Water Footprint of Food," Grace Communications Foundation, 2018. http://www.gracelinks.org/1361/the-water-footprint-of-food
10. "The Disappearing Rainforest," http://www.savetheamazon.org/rainforeststats.htm
11. John Roach, "Seafood May Be Gone by 2048, Study Says," *National Geographic News,* November 2006. http://news.nationalgeographic.com/news/2006/11/061102-seafood-threat.html
12. "Meat-eater's Guide to Climate Change and Health," Environmental Working Group, 2011. http://static.ewg.org/reports/2011/meateaters/pdf/methodology_ewg_meat_eaters_guide_to_health_and_climate_2011.pdf
13. John Robbins, "The Truth About Grass-fed Beef," December 2012. https://foodrevolution.org/blog/the-truth-about-grassfed-beef/
14. "10 Rainforest Facts for 2018," Mongabay Rainforests. http://rainforests.mongabay.com/facts/rainforest-facts.html#8
15. "Measuring the Daily Destruction of the World's Rainforests," EarthTalk, *Scientific American.* https://www.scientificamerican.com/article/earth-talks-daily-destruction/
16. "U.S. could feed 800 million people with grain that livestock eat, Cornell ecologist advises animal scientists," *Cornell Chronicle,* August 1997. http://www.news.cornell.edu/stories/1997/08/us-could-feed-800-million-people-grain-livestock-eat
17. Robert Thurman, *The Jewel Tree of Tibet* (New York: Simon & Schuster, 2005), p. 111.

# Born to this World
## a Bodhisattva

ALAN DALE

My childhood was full of animals. Our house in the country was surrounded by farms with animals and fields of wilderness with an abundance of wild animals. One of the few business-es in the area was a large wholesale pet supply company that had warehouses of just about every animal you could ever imag-ine that could be a pet. Both of my parents worked there. This place would occasionally discard live animals into the dumpster if they were deemed not sellable. Being a curious child, those thrown away beings would often end up rescued by me and taken home for care.

When I was an infant, my mother would sit my highchair facing the large family aquarium and I would watch the various aquatic beings swimming about in the tank. This would go on for hours almost every day for a better part of my early life. Often my consciousness would eventually project itself into this wondrous world. What I mean by this is that the center point of my consciousness was no longer operating from the viewpoint of my body, but from the viewpoint of the various creatures swimming about in the water. I would become aware of the world through the senses of the fish, shrimp, eel, sea horse, or turtle.

As I grew up and started walking on two feet I would use this same technique with other beings such as the cats, dogs, horses, chickens, cows, and goats. I also had a large menagerie of wild critters that I would catch in the nearby fields and countryside as temporary pets, eventually to be released back to the wild. I understood that there was not much difference between how I experienced the world versus how they experienced the world. The main difference was their viewpoint and their way of understanding.

This projection of consciousness was, as I now understand, an aspect of a yogic process called *samyama* which is a combined simultaneous practice of *dharana* (concentration), *dhyana* (meditation) and *samadhi* (union). It is a term summarizing the combined process of psychological absorption in the object of meditation. It starts as a witness state leading to mindfulness, and then eventually leading to transcendence. These transcendent experiences started in my childhood and have continued to this day.

These mystical episodes led me to explore and study comparative religions, various spiritual traditions, altered states of consciousness, and different yoga and meditation practices. This brought me eventually to a spiritual group in my teens called informally "the meeting of the mystics." Here I met the poet Allen

Ginsberg who then introduced me to Chogyam Trungpa, a meditation master and holder of the Kagyu and Nyingma lineages in Tibetan Buddhism. I became a disciple of Trungpa Rinpoche, and later became a lama in the Kagyu, Nyingma, and Gelug lineages. My teachers have included the Dalai Lama, Khensur Rinpoche, Choden Rinpoche, Garchen Rinpoche, and Chetsang Rinpoche.

**Not Killing Other Beings**
Butcher day on the farms were the most ominous and dreaded times of my early life. Oh, how I hated those days and would try to disappear and hide. In those times, farmers would often butcher and prepare the carcasses for the ice trucks to take to market. The day would be focused on a particular species, with chickens, cows, and pigs being the most common. Everyone on the farm would participate along with neighbors and nearby kinsfolk. Everyone young and old would be assigned a task, part of the assembly line of duties to be performed. Many of the tasks were repetitive and people would trade tasks to relieve the monotony.

I remember the first time I was deemed old enough to participate in the butchery. It was chicken day and all the chickens were in stacks of wired cages waiting near the chopping block. I was first told to watch and learn how it was done. I could not believe the horror of what I was witnessing. I wondered why humans were so primitive, cruel and nonchalant about killing these poor chicken beings. It was just the day before that I was feeding and playing with these very same chickens. These chickens were joyful and innocent, and were my friends. Now these doomed chickens were meeting their end of life, cut short by the hunger of humans.

After observing the madness for a while it was then my turn to chop the heads off the chickens with an axe. The axe was covered in blood and put into my shaking hands. First, I was tasked with a test run by chopping a thick twig in two. Then, one of the assistants grabbed a live chicken and held the body down on the chopping block with her neck exposed. The air was full of the overwhelming smell of wet feathers from the blood of prior deaths and everything repulsed me to the core of my being. Next to the chopping block was a basket of chopped off heads from the previous victims.

When chickens are on the chopping block, they are not quiet. They often seemed to be pleading for their lives. When the axe falls, the head pops off and blood spurts everywhere. The head falls into the basket with the eyes still wide open and moving about. The beak is still moving but there are no more cries for help to be heard. The headless body is still very active and, if it gets away, it can run for a long distance.

When my eye met the eye of the chicken on the death block with her body struggling, her sounds of panic, and her rapid breathing, my heart stopped and I felt the soul of the chicken. I instantly recognized that this was one of the chickens I was happily playing with the day before. I dropped the axe to my side and took off running like a bolt of lightening. I had no idea where I was running to but ended up in a nearby house where I hid until sun down. From that day forth, refraining from killing or harming other beings would be central to my spiritual practice.

**Meat as Addictive Poison**

My mother would often take me to doctors to determine the cause of my chronic childhood sickness. When doctors could not find a cause, they often labeled me as an overly sensitive child. Later in my teens one doctor made a discovery after getting some blood test results back from the lab. He was convinced that I was suffering from small doses of poison over time. He could not determine the type or cause of poisoning so he sent me to a blood specialist who had five doctorate degrees in fields relating to the study of blood.

After many tests and microscope analyses of my blood, the specialist discovered the source and reason for my poisoning. It was meat and animal products. Basically, whenever my white blood cells were exposed to meat or animal products in the bloodstream they would explode. The exploding white blood cells caused a phenomenon resulting in the creation of toxic biochemicals that were highly addictive. The more I consumed animal products the more I became addicted and craved meat.

During the era in which I grew up, it was a common belief that if you did not eat meat you would die. Where else would we get our protein, if not from meat, dairy and eggs? People did not understand that protein is in virtually everything we eat, and that eating a balanced plant-based diet provides plenty of high-quality protein. Nor did they understand the mechanics of food addiction and how certain foods create chemicals in the body to which one can become dependent.

My mother was shocked to discover that it was the meat, eggs and dairy that were making me deathly sick. Not only that, but the blood specialist explained that most everyone has a food addiction to some degree or another to meat, eggs or dairy. She explained that it is an adaptation for humans to tolerate animal products. Humans do not need to adapt to a plant-based diet because it is the natural diet for humans. Stopping meat and dairy consumption abruptly can thus be potentially dangerous, like detoxing from any addictive substance too quickly. There can be serious withdrawal symptoms.

Once I stopped consuming meat and became vegetarian my health greatly improved and I was no longer a sickly child. Later I adopted a completely plant-based diet that made me not only healthier physically but also emotionally, mentally and spiritually. This diet has had a significant impact on my spiritual growth and on developing compassion for other beings. A vegan diet is estimated to spare about 200 animal lives per year. I've discovered that once totally off animal products, most of us will eventually stop craving them and if eaten by accident, we may even feel repulsed or get ill.

## Buddha Says, "Stop Meat Eating"

The first precept of Buddhism is abstaining from causing harm and taking life, both human and non-human. There is no better way to meet this precept than to follow a vegan lifestyle. Meat eating is rejected by the Buddha in such sutras as the *Angulimaliya*, *Hastikakshya*, the *Mahamegha*, the *Nirvana*, and the *Lankavatara*.

In the *Lankavatara Sutra*, the Buddha states that meat is not agreeable to the wise. It has a nauseating odor, it causes a bad reputation, it is food for the carnivorous and it is not to be eaten. To those who eat meat there are detrimental effects, and to those who do not, merits accrue. We should know that meat-eaters bring detrimental effects upon themselves.

The Buddha also states that from eating meat, arrogance is born. From arrogance, erroneous imaginations arise, and from these imaginations greed is born. For this reason, one should refrain from eating meat. By greed the mind becomes stupefied; there is attachment to stupefaction and there is no emancipation from birth and death.

Meat is the food of ordinary people, but is rejected by the noble and the spiritual. Meat consumption is wholly destitute of virtue. It is not the food on which the wise sustain themselves. The Buddha asked, "How could I permit my followers to taste of such unwholesome and unfitting nourishment as meat?"

Nowhere in the Mahayana sutras is meat expressly permitted, nor is it referred to as proper among the foods prescribed for the Buddha's followers. Bodhisattvas, who are ever desirous of purity in their discipline, should wholly refrain from eating meat. As the Buddha said, "Eating meat destroys the attitude of great compassion."

## Awakening the Heart through Veganism

The ultimate authority beyond the Buddha is that of Buddhist wisdom or *prajna*. This wisdom, or insight into the nature of reality, emanates from the universal heart-mind and leads us toward *nirvana.* We can obtain this wisdom directly from our own heart that is no longer obscured. The path of a bodhisattva is to uncover the wisdom hidden within the heart. The companion of *prajna* is compassion, *karuna,* the direct path to uncovering wisdom.

*Bodhicitta* is the altruistic wish to obtain enlightenment for the benefit of all living beings. It is the consciousness of compassion. Along with the understanding of emptiness, bodhicitta is one of the two essentials for treading the path to enlightenment. Without the motivating force of altruistic intention, understanding emptiness is not sufficient for one to make progress on the spiritual path. Bodhicitta is thus considered the essential root of the path.

The first *chakra* to be developed within the womb is the heart chakra. It is the portal from which consciousness and all the other chakras are born, and the last chakra from which consciousness withdraws upon death. We are to cherish the heart and the hearts of others. All beings intuitively know what will help their heart grow and also what will diminish the sacred sensitivity that we all possess but often ignore. If we nurture the heart, the heart will nurture us.

The best way to nurture one's heart is to be of service to others and to recognize that we are all interconnected. By harming others, we harm ourselves. Service has a cumulative effect depending upon our actions. By consciously refraining from harming or paying others to harm animals, we will over time generate a more loving and sensitive awareness that accumulates good merit and karma.

Good merit transpires into the capacity for deeper understanding of ourselves, and leads to ever-deepening wisdom. This wisdom is universal heart wisdom. There is no greater path than that of cultivating a compassionate heart.

## Higher Yoga Practices Require a Vegan Diet
Advanced yogis have observed that what they eat can have a

profound effect on their meditation. In Ayurvedic scriptures, the primary force of life is composed of three qualities or principles called *gunas*. The three gunas are *sattva* (tranquil or subtle energy), *rajas* (active energy) and *tamas* (inertia or dullness). Sattvic food is always fresh, natural, plant-sourced and organic with little to no processing, freshly cooked or raw and perhaps lightly seasoned. It is wholesome food consisting of nourishing carbohydrates, proteins, fiber, vitamins, and other nutrients. Animal products fall under rajasic and tamasic foods. These foods are considered to be of a lower vibration and should be avoided by yogis.

A sattvic diet will make a sattvic person; it is the diet of a bodhisattva. Sattvic individuals are loving and pure-minded. They feel compassion for all expressions of life and face life events positively. Sattvic people have effective control over their emotions. It's hard to make them upset or angry easily. Sattvic people most often look alert, aware, and full of luster and are recognized for their wisdom, happiness, and inner peace. Sattvic individuals do not easily fatigue mentally. Their meditation and sleep quality is better, so they get good rest even if they sleep for a fewer number of hours.

Generally speaking, the lower one's resting breath rate, the more likely one will obtain advanced spiritual experiences. The average resting breath rate for an adult is usually between 12-18 breaths per minute (BPM). If one is unhealthy, it can be anywhere between 19-25 BPM. Any higher than this usually means, as an adult, you are suffering and probably dying. Meditation and yoga practice teach a yogi to breathe more deeply and slowly bringing one's BPM down. Their resting breath rate is usually between 8-11 BPM and for advanced yogis it can be 4-7 BPM.

As we find ways to lower our resting breath rate, we will notice how much easier it is to get into more advanced states of meditation. There are numerous ways to naturally to do this but the most important way is to eliminate all things that create physical, emotional, mental and spiritual stress. An easy way to address all four is to switch to a plant-based diet.

The next step is to explore beyond the mind-body complex. There are layers or dimensions of this complex that are not apparent but can be discovered through advanced yogic practices, revealed by working with the channels, energy-winds, and vital essence. It is the task of the yogi to employ appropriate methods to understand the depths of the subtle fields beyond the physical. It is difficult to make progress when the ingestion of animal substances obscures our ability to sense the subtle aspects of our vital essence.

## Veganism and Spirituality Go Hand in Hand

Spirituality is the quality of being aware of spiritual or eternal consciousness, as opposed to material or physical forms. Being vegan includes respecting the consciousness of others and ourselves, through refraining from eating, wearing, or causing harm to them. Can we call ourselves spiritual without such respect?

We don't know what we're doing when we turn a blind eye to spirituality. Eating animal-based foods desensitizes us and we lose the ability to empathize with others. We suppress the inclination to go beyond our self-focus or selfishness.

There is hope for us to become more conscious of what is obvious. The first step is to stop making excuses for our behavior. By recognizing it for what it is and taking responsibility, we can make positive changes. Ignorance will not save us. Life is shorter than we think so we can start now.

We can commit to making an effort to minimize harm to others, starting with what we eat. We can measure what we eat by how much suffering went into creating our meal. The less suffering we are responsible for, the more we will progress on the path of compassion. Eventually we may become a bodhisattva or accomplished yogi.

We can take it further and try looking at our suffering footprint on a daily basis. Besides what we eat, what do we consume in the way of products or services that caused harm to others? What about our actions or inactions that may cause suffering? What about harsh words, or kind words that we fail to utter? May we all, brothers and sisters, become enlightened for the benefit of all sentient beings.

# Dark Alleys and Bright Aisles

TASHI NYIMA

~~~~~~~~~~~~~~~~~~~~~~~~~~~~~~~~~~~~~~~~~~~~~~~~~~~~~~~~~~~~~~~~~~~~

*Having abandoned the taking of life, refraining from the taking of life, we dwell without violence, with the knife laid down—scrupulous, full of mercy—trembling with compassion for all sentient beings.*

- Buddha Shakyamuni

When people think of Buddhist monks, if they think of us at all, they imagine that we dwell in clouds of incense, smiling serenely, unperturbed, meditating on nothing. But, as you just read, we are not called to drift placidly in emptiness, but to "tremble with compassion for all sentient beings."

I thought that the mention of 'trembling' was just a rhetorical device, until late one night, returning with my teacher from visiting with refugees, we passed by a dark alley and heard the cries of fear and pain of a youth who was being beaten by a group of five men.

Without hesitation, my teacher approached the men, and smiling broadly, asked them if it would not be "much more fun" to beat up two Buddhist monks instead of one young man. I was not smiling broadly. I was not smiling at all. You see, Buddhist monks vow not to resort to violence, even to defend ourselves. We do not fight. This did not look good at all. Here we were, two pacifists in robes. We were going to get pummeled.

Surprisingly, the beating stopped, the men laughed nervously, uttered some choice profanities, and left. Perhaps they imagined we were Shaolin monks, ready to rain our secret Kung Fu moves on them...

After making sure that the young man was safe and in the care of emergency responders, I asked my teacher if he had known that we would not come to harm.

He responded that he did not, but at the very least, we could have taken some of the blows, and not all would have fallen on that one young man.

And then he told me soberly that it was our duty, when confronted with suffering, to *get in the way*, to stand between those who harm and those who are hurt.

Not all abuse happens in dark alleys. Much unspeakable cruelty takes place in the brightly lit aisles where we purchase the flesh of animals, their eggs, their milk, their skin, their wool, their feathers, and their fur. Those brightly lit aisles conceal the horrible darkness where animals are confined, enslaved, tortured, raped, and slaughtered for our pleasure. I will not share with you the gory details, but the awful truth is there for you to see, as plain as day.

What makes some beings worthy of compassion, while others seem to merit only our disdain? Is it their intelligence? Is it the ability to speak? Is it the actions we perform? Are we not called to feel compassion for the dull, the dumb, the infirm, and the disabled? Beings are worthy of compassion because they are sentient; they suffer and they feel pain.

If we killed human beings at the same rate that we kill other animals, we humans would be extinct in a mere seventeen days. To desire peace in a world in which only human lives matter is not only hypocritical, it is also destructive.

To want to reduce the suffering of human beings *only* is nothing but extended selfishness. There will be no world, and no community, unless we stop the enslavement, torture, and slaughter of billions of land and marine animals every year.

If we feel no compassion for the plight of suffering animals, we can at least consider the pain we inflict upon ourselves and future human generations. Animal agriculture is the single largest contributor to climate destabilization, water pollution and depletion, deforestation, species extinction, human disease, and human hunger. What we do unto non-human animals, we do unto ourselves.

I implore everyone to look upon our fellow sentient beings, human and non-human, with compassion. If we cannot prevent the cruelty they suffer, at least let harm not be inflicted for our pleasure, paid for with our money, and executed in our name.

We cannot speak sincerely of loving kindness and compassion while confining, abusing, and slaughtering our fellow sentient beings. Compassion begins in our hearts, but it manifests in our shopping carts, in our closets, in our kitchens, and on our plates.

First among the moral injunctions, accepted and shared by all schools and lineages of the Buddha Dharma, is the precept to abstain from taking life (*Anguttara Agama*):

*I undertake the precept to refrain from destroying living creatures.*

*A disciple of the Noble Ones, abandoning the taking of life, abstains from taking life. In doing so, he gives freedom from danger, freedom from animosity, freedom from oppression to limitless numbers of beings. In giving freedom from danger, freedom from animosity, freedom from oppression to limitless numbers of beings, he gains a share in limitless freedom from danger, freedom from animosity, and freedom from oppression.*

*This is the first gift, the first great gift —original, long-standing, traditional, ancient, untainted, unadulterated from the beginning— that is not open to suspicion, will never be open to suspicion, and is praised by knowledgeable contemplatives and sages.*

Is this injunction to abstain from killing solely inclusive of humans? The Buddha gives this instruction in the *Griha Vinaya* (Rules for Householders, *Dharmika Sutra, Kshudraka Agama*):

*Let him not destroy, or cause to be destroyed, any life at all, or sanction the acts of those who do so. Let him refrain even from hurting any creature, both those that are strong and those that tremble in the world.*

If we fail to understand the universality of this injunction, the Buddha clarifies (*Kshudraka Agama*):

*Whether they be creatures of the land or air, whoever harms here any living being,*
*Who has no compassion for all that live, let such a one be known as depraved.*

And in the *Anguttara Agama*:

*I am a friend of the footless, I am a friend of all bipeds,
    I am a friend of those with four feet, I am a
friend of the many-footed.*
        *...*
    *May all creatures, all breathing things, all be-
ings one and all, without exception, experience good
fortune only. May they not fall into any harm.*

Should we intend to skirt the First Precept by claiming
innocence of the deed if others do the killing for us? He adds
(*Kshudraka Agama*):

*We should not kill any living beings, nor cause them
to be killed, nor should we incite any other to kill. Do
never injure any being, whether strong or weak, in this
entire universe!*

In the *Brahmajala Sutra*, the Buddha says to His disciples,
confirming the primacy of the First Precept:

*Abandoning the taking of life, the ascetic Gauta-
ma dwells refraining from taking life, without stick
or sword, scrupulous, compassionate, trembling for
the welfare of all living beings. Thus the householder
should praise the Tathagata.*

And in the *Dhammapada* (*Udanavarga*):

*The one who has left all violence, who never harms any
beings at all, whether they are moving or still, who
neither kills, nor causes to kill, such a one, harmless, is
the Holy One!*

Innumerable statements proclaiming the primacy of the First Principle can be found throughout the Theravada and Mahayana canons of Buddhist scripture. The Mahayana sutras, in particular, are unequivocal in their censure both of killing animals and consuming their flesh and other products:

*A disciple of the Buddha must maintain a mind of kindness and cultivate the practice of liberating beings. He should reflect thus:*

*"All male beings have been my father and all females have been my mother. There is not a single being that has not given birth to me during my previous lives; hence, all beings of the Six Realms are my parents.*

*"Therefore, when a person kills and eats any of these beings, he thereby slaughters my parents. Furthermore, he kills a body that was once my own, for all elemental earth and water previously served as part of my body, and all elemental fire and wind have served as my basic substance.*

*"Therefore, I shall always cultivate the practice of liberating beings and in every life be reborn in the eternally abiding Dharma, and teach others to liberate beings as well."*

*Whenever a Bodhisattva sees a person preparing to kill animals, he should devise a skillful method to rescue and protect them, freeing them from their suffering and difficulties.*

—Buddha Shakyamuni, *Brahmajala Sutra*

In an attempt to justify their appetite for the flesh and blood of animals, some individuals allege that (1) the Buddha permitted the consumption of meat under three conditions, (2) vegetarians are "the sons of the infamous Devadatta", and (3) the Buddha himself ate meat. These are patently specious claims.

The Pali text of the *Jivaka Sutta*, the putative source of the infamous 'three purities' argument, states:

> *I say that there are three instances in which meat should not be eaten: when it is seen, heard, or suspected. I say that meat should not be eaten in those three instances.*
>
> *I say that there are three instances in which meat may be eaten: when it is not seen, not heard, and not suspected. I say that meat may be eaten in these three instances.*

Clearly, the Buddha is stipulating here that if a monk inadvertently consumes meat that has been placed in his begging bowl, he is not at fault. His action is pure. However, if he sees, hears, or even suspects that there is animal flesh in his bowl, he must not eat it.

Later commentators calculatingly inserted the phrase "that the living being has been slaughtered for oneself" after each repetition of the word 'suspected.' The phrase does not appear in the original Pali text. It is a spurious addition, making it seem as if the Buddha allowed his monks to eat meat when the animal was not expressly killed to feed them, or at least when they did not see, hear, or suspect it.

This interpolation is linguistically unwarranted. More importantly, it contradicts the unequivocal teaching of the Buddha on the matter. The Buddha gives extensive arguments against meat-eating in the *Angulimaliya Sutra*, *Nirvana Sutra*, *Karma Sutra*, *Shurangama Sutra*, *Mahamegha Sutra*, *Lankavatara Sutra*, *Mahaparinirvana Sutra*, and others.

In the *Brahmajala Sutra*, the Buddha Shakyamuni clearly exhorts his followers to adopt strict adherence to non-harming:

*Should you willingly and knowingly eat flesh, you defile yourselves.*

*Pray, let us not consume any flesh or whatsoever comes from sentient beings.*

In order to preserve a counterfeit harmony, some persons hold that the Buddha instructed us to be silent in the face of blatant misrepresentations of the Dharma, such as this deceptive reasoning of those who pretend that the cruel enslavement, exploitation, and slaughter of animals is approved by the Buddha if we "do not see, hear, or suspect" that the animals were killed expressly for our sake.

Such persons place the temporary emotional discomfort of their 'Dharma teachers' and sangha peers over the unspeakable suffering of non-human animals. This complicit timidity is contrary to the Dharma.

The Buddha said in the Middle Length Discourses:

*Such speech as the Tathagata knows to be true, correct, and beneficial, even if unwelcome and disagreeable to others, the Tathagata knows the time to use such speech.*

*...*

*Why is that? Because the Tathagata has compassion for all beings.*

Another tired and tiresome argument trotted out insistently by those who would misrepresent the Dharma to justify their lust for flesh and blood is the refusal of the Buddha Shakyamuni to accept the so-called "Five Rules of Devadatta."

The five rules proposed by Devadatta were that monks reside only in the forest, that they depend exclusively on begging, that robes be made from discarded rags, that they dwell under trees, and that they abstain from eating flesh.

These rules were meant to convey the appearance that Devadatta was more austere than the Buddha Shakyamuni, and therefore a more apt leader for the Sangha. In the *Cullavagga Sutta*, chapter 7, where Devadatta's intentions are made explicitly clear, Devadatta says to one of his co-conspirators: "It is possible with these five items to make a schism in the recluse Gautama's Order, a breaking of the concord. For, your reverence, people esteem austerity."

There are three reasons why the Buddha rejected Devadatta's "five rules" and none had to do with the merits of the proposal on abstaining from flesh:

1. Devadatta's concerns were not ethical; they were strictly political. His intention was to split the Sangha and advance his craving for fame and power.
2. The rules of the *Vinaya* were developed progressively, and always in response to specific doubts or conflicts. They were never issued a *priori*.
3. The rule concerning the consumption of flesh was redundant, as it was already covered in the very first of the Five Precepts, as well as in innumerable injunctions.

Perhaps the most infamous of all justifications for flesh consumption is the claim that the Buddha ate meat, and that he died from eating contaminated pork. The term used in the (Pali) *Mahaparinibbana Sutta* to describe the dish that was served to the Buddha at his last meal is *sukara-maddava*, which literally means "pig's delight," a clear reference to a type of mushroom that pigs are keen to eat. The Pali term for pig meat is *sukara-mamsa*.

Carolyn Rhys-Davids, who served from 1923 to 1942 as president of the Pali Text Society, clearly noted the faulty translation more than seven decades ago, but proponents of carnivorism still trot out this fallacy today. Unless one is grossly ignorant of the Pali language, or is willfully misleading others, it is impossible to assert that "pigs' delight" means "pork meat," as if the Buddha had ordered a fanciful dish at a modern Chinese-American restaurant.

> *Let a person not give credence to the many rationalizations given to justify animal flesh eating. What word-jugglers say under the influence of their addictive craving for animal flesh is sophistic, delusional, and argumentative.*

—Buddha Shakyamuni, Mahaparinirvana Sutra

If these words have made you uncomfortable, please ask yourself why. I humbly stand before you, as the Buddha instructed, trembling with compassion for you and for all sentient beings.

# The Beckoning Path

Will Tuttle

〰〰〰〰〰〰〰〰〰〰〰〰〰〰〰〰〰〰〰〰〰〰〰〰〰〰〰〰〰〰

*"Flesh free from the three objections, not prepared,*
*unasked, unsolicited, there is none.*
*Therefore one should not eat flesh."*

—Arya Shantideva

Although we are now at the end of our literary journey together, we are also in the beginning stages of contributing to a more mutually-inspiring relationship between veganism and Buddhism. Like most religions, Buddhism is a system of teachings aiming to assist its adherents to evolve spiritually. The underlying idea is that as we cultivate our awareness and awaken spiritually, we naturally help to bring healing and harmony not just to ourselves, but also to our society. Spirituality transcends the particularities of religion, history, and culture, and addresses the dimension of ourselves that is consciousness, and that is not essentially separate from other beings. Spiritual awareness, whatever the religious or non-religious trappings may be, naturally gives rise to compassion for others, including animals, and also to ethical behavior because it's the lived realization that beings are not merely material objects, but are conscious and sentient manifestations of life inherently deserving of respect.

Animal agriculture is the antithesis of spirituality. It reduces beings to the status of harvestable commodities, stealing their sovereignty through routine sexual abuse, mutilation, and death. This destroys not just their lives, purposes, and happiness, but undermines ours as well. It fosters a desensitized awareness focused on separateness, denial, entitlement, competition, and consumerism. Our freedom is eroded by enslaving animals. Herderism, the core organizing principle of our society for the past ten thousand years, suppresses spiritual awareness in individuals and in our cultural institutions, including our religious institutions. Through acculturation, this has become invisible to us.

When we have religious teachings, practices, and teachers that do not question animal agriculture and eating animal-sourced foods, we have religions that lack spirituality and that tend, ironically, to reduce spiritual awareness in individuals and society as a whole, while contributing to delusion, injustice, and war. The four core practices of animal agriculture are mentally reducing beings to mere material objects; enslaving them from birth to death; sexually abusing them and stealing their offspring;

and pre-meditatively killing all of them. On every level—physically, cognitively, emotionally, sexually, spiritually, culturally, and ethically—animal agriculture undermines our sensitivity and awareness, and promotes materialism and the exploitation of the weak by the strong. The fact that it is so wide-spread, deeply-rooted, and generally accepted makes its relentlessly devastating effects virtually untrackable to their source, even to those of us who consider ourselves to be spiritually oriented.

Because all of us have been raised in a culture organized at its core around herding animals for food, we have been wounded from birth by the medical, educational, religious, familial, economic, and governmental institutions compelling us to participate in animal agriculture. When we eat animal foods, we are not only harming our physical health. We are also eating attitudes that reduce our psychological, cultural, and spiritual wellness. Food is our most intimate connection with nature and with our culture, and being required from infancy to eat foods of terror and toxicity suppresses our innate wisdom and sense of connectedness with the other intriguing and beautiful expressions of life on this Earth. Herderism, because it requires and ritually indoctrinates both desensitization and disconnectedness, reduces our capacities to care, feel, and make connections, eroding our ability to understand the cause of suffering.

We have been told from childhood that hot dogs, hamburgers, cheese, eggs, and fish sticks are our tasty friends, giving us needed protein, calcium, and other health benefits, and that ranching and fishing are natural and noble activities that help to feed us and keep our world healthy. Fortunately, we are waking up from this erroneous narrative and realizing that our friendly foods, and the industries based on animal exploitation, are actually our deadliest enemies, as cows, pigs, and chickens have certainly long realized. They harm every dimension of our health relentlessly, but this reality—and our capacity to awaken and understand it—is suppressed by all our social institutions.

Religion is the social institution that is perhaps best suited to upholding ethical standards and demanding protection of the weak, but it is also the most divided and compromised by two competing loyalties. It has a mission to support and transmit the prevailing cultural norms and values from generation to generation, but it also has a second mission, which is to encourage the spiritual impulse in people. Spirituality, however, has no such divided loyalty, and propels us only to discover our true nature, even if it means questioning cultural narratives and norms. Spirituality easily recognizes the pig in the bacon, the cow in the cheese, and the injustice and trauma that we are causing by eating these foods and feeding them to our children. Spirituality categorically rejects this unnecessary violence and calls for an awakening from the abusive behavior as well as from the underlying materialism and reductionism that enable and inform animal agriculture.

This is the great tension between spirituality and religion. Spirituality can never condone the culturally-approved practices of animal exploitation and abuse for food, clothing, entertainment, research, or any purpose because it is rooted in respecting the interconnectedness and unity of life and consciousness. It is not concerned, as religion is, with supporting the existing cultural traditions and values. Spirituality includes animals because they are endowed with sentience as we humans are. Thus, teachers and teachings are fully spiritual when they explicitly renounce all forms of animal agriculture, animal-sourced foods and products, and other forms of animal abuse. There may be religious teachers who do not question animal agriculture because their primary aim is to maintain the prevailing cultural narratives, be popular and be financially successful. However, as soon as spirituality comes into play, materialism and practices of exploitation are vigorously questioned and abandoned, and replaced by teachings that cultivate respect, kindness, and freedom for all.

Buddhism seems to have begun as a fully spiritual teaching in this sense, questioning injustice and violence, and helped shift the ancient Indian culture away from the practice of animal sacrifice and toward vegan living based on respect for all. This may have been somewhat easier at that time because Indian cuisine was more organized around plant-based foods then, except for the practice, apparently brought by ancient immigrants from Egypt and central Asia, of exploiting cows for their milk. When Buddhism later spread to east Asian countries like China, Korea, Japan, and Vietnam, which had no tradition of using cows for milk, the Buddhist teachings and teachers evolved to explicitly encourage vegan living, a practice continuing to this day.

Buddhism, rooted as it is in *ahimsa*, has thus been an often hidden thread in the centuries-old tapestry of vegetarianism and veganism as they have evolved throughout the world to the present day. As the authors in this volume have demonstrated and discussed, both Buddhism and veganism are living, transformational forces in peoples' lives. The gift that veganism brings is the insistence on practicing *ahimsa* in daily life by explicitly including animals within our sphere of mindful caring and kindness. However, veganism lacks a foundation in cultivating deeper awareness, inner stillness and receptivity. As vegans, we can fall prey to despair and anger because of our unique and still unaccepted orientation, and may become mired in depression, anger, or alienation, or in blaming, shaming, and criticizing behaviors that are harmful to us and to our cause. Buddhism brings the gift of mindfulness and the cultivation of meditative awareness, and though Buddhism has a strong foundation in *ahimsa*, this has been watered down in many cases due to the usual influences of corruption, convenience, conformism, fear, hubris, taste, ambition, hypocrisy, and sloth. Just as vegan practice can bring an essential clarity and accountability to Buddhist practice, Buddhist practice can bring depth, mindfulness, and resilience to vegan practice. Together, they can contribute to co-creating a more comprehensive framework for both personal and social transformation.

For example, a primary danger for Buddhist practitioners is sometimes referred to as "Zen sickness," which is a dull, pseudo-serenity in which our routinized meditation and way of thinking keep us stuck in a detached, enforced calmness. Buddhist practice calls us to an awakening out of any enforced mental state to full aliveness and responsiveness in the moment-to-moment awareness of our lives. Eating animal foods dulls our sensitivities. Mindful vegan living can help reconnect us with the purity, passion, joy, and aliveness that our cultural wounds have repressed, and reconnect us with the compassion and awareness that have been covered over by years of indoctrination in narratives of repression.

On the other hand, even as veganism continues to grow, some of us try to justify eating animal foods because we tell ourselves we are bringing the Buddhist practice of mindfulness to our non-vegan meals. Not far from where we live in northern California, for example, there's a local slaughter facility advertising that it provides "mindful meats." This humane-washing and co-opting of Buddhist terms and ideas is readily apparent. We would never consider promoting mindful raping, mindful stealing, mindful harming, and so forth, because mindfulness is the antithesis of these behaviors. Mindfulness is the cultivation of awareness, and to willfully abuse others requires that our awareness be submerged beneath a distorting narrative that rationalizes toxic attitudes and behavior. Buddhist practice is an effort to liberate our minds from the narratives that hold us in delusion and cause violence. Veganism is clearly a helpful ally in this effort.

The world's religions promote the Golden Rule of *ahimsa*, and yet virtually all of them, even Buddhism and Jainism that seem to champion it, continue to be hijacked into justifying violence toward animals by the pervasive and prevailing demands of animal agriculture as the core organizing principle of our planetary culture. As we as individuals make efforts to awaken from the cultural trance of herderism and routinized animal abuse, our transformation is our contribution to our collective transformation, helping our spiritual and religious communities reclaim their authentic foundations. We liberate animals from the violence of "mindful meats" and liberate Buddhism from this violence to its teachings as well, freeing it to illuminate and inspire compassion and liberation for all as originally intended.

We live in challenging times. Animal agriculture continues to devastate our Earth's ecosystems, our culture's harmony and sanity, and our physical health. More insidiously, it also erodes our cultural and personal intelligence, and our awareness, empathy, and creativity. Our short-term future is in question at this point. It's well understood that we could go extinct soon, without, ironically, ever understanding why it happened. The vegan dimensions of many traditions of wisdom, including Buddhism, have been repressed for too long under the strident din of animal agriculture's narrative of domination, greed, and elitism.

Nevertheless, by opening our eyes and looking deeply, we can discern a bright and beckoning path that leads to a doorway into a positive future. Increasing numbers of us are being called to this path and are calling others to join us. There is nothing objectively stopping us from collectively proceeding along this bright path to new dimensions of peace, abundance, and freedom. Fear, delusion, attachment, and conformism are the primary obstacles.

As mentioned in this book's introduction, virtually all traditions of Buddhism (and of most religions as well) are open to becoming more explicit about the essential importance that a commitment to respect and kindness for animals has in their teachings. Each of us can contribute in our unique way to this opening of awareness about the universality and primacy of the vegan message. We are called to more fully embody the values of kindness in the crucible of our relationships, with all kinds of animals, including the most difficult ones, humans. It is through congruence and transparency that living truths are transmitted.

The Earth we inhabit is beautiful and abundant, and can easily feed and support all of us. When we awaken from the consumerist trance of animal agriculture, the land and waters will heal, along with our minds, bodies, relationships, and communities. This is the vision of engaged and caring awareness and action implicit in Buddhism and veganism. Buddhist teachings call for vegan living, and vegan living calls for the same awakening from deluded narratives toward which Buddhist practice aims. May we succeed in our efforts to bring awakening to ourselves and our world, for the benefit of all beings.

**References:**
1.    Will Tuttle, The World Peace Diet (New York: Lantern), 2016, Tenth Anniversary Edition. See Chapter Two, "Our Culture's Roots."

# May All Life Be Loved

Master Ma Chuo

In July of 2012, walking in the Lashingbu Mountains of Tibet, at about 16,000 feet, I found myself under a sky so bright and clear it seemed to have just been wiped by a pair of gentle hands. A cloud was lightly floating by above, like a playful child, jumping in front of the blazing sun, as if reaching out to cover the sun's brilliant eyes. It tiptoed over and gently kissed the sun. The sunlight streamed around the cloud's soft back, dappling it and sending shadows rising and falling among the rolling hills. On the mountainside, a brisk breeze spun ephemeral music of earth and heaven.

I was standing on a flat slope, breathing in peace, and feeling immersed in the healing beauty of blueness, light, and freshness that slowly filled my lungs. A warm current went through my whole body. This nourishing stream of nature's living vitality brought tears to my eyes. I had longed for this in my dreams.

Not far away, the local people were unrolling their new Sutra streamers and hanging them on the beckoning hillside. I joined them, and after tying and attaching all the streamers that I had in my hands, I put my palms together, lowered my gaze, closed my eyes, and prayed for the well-being of all living beings, yearning for the gentle breeze to carry my wishes into every direction and every dimension.

I lost track of time, being immersed in my inward meditation. Upon opening my eyes, the sunlight was fading. Looking up, I realized it was time to head back down, but I wasn't sure of the way. I suddenly felt a little flustered. Standing alone in the thin mountain air, I began to feel oxygen deprived and this made me even more anxious. I looked around and searched for someone who could give me directions.

A rustling sound gave me some hope in my trepidation. A white-bearded Tibetan antelope slowly appeared in front of me from behind some bushes and I was overjoyed. The antelope knew this wild mountain landscape and would certainly be able to help me find my way down the mountain. I thought I would have a good talk with him.

I waved my hand with excitement and greeted the antelope loudly as if seeing an old friend in my hometown. "Brother Antelope, how are you? Sorry to disturb you from grass grazing! Excuse me."

"Little Moustache," as I called him, raised his eyes and made eye contact with me. It felt right.

"Brother Antelope how are you? Could you take me down the hill, please? I'm lost."

"Little Moustache" saw my concerned face and walked up to me. The Tibetan antelope turned slowly and seemed to understand my appeal. He walked past me, and kept grazing as he wandered down the hill. I followed him and recited a Heart Sutra for him. I told him the story of my ongoing walk to spread the vegan message all over China, sometimes even drawing quite close to him. We went down the mountain together in the style of an antelope followed by a man. Eventually, after going through a low cave, we finally reached a relatively flat slope. Overjoyed, I realized that now I wasn't far from the next village where I could spend the night.

"Brother Antelope, thank you for taking me down. If you can understand what I'm saying, give me a kiss."

I closed my eyes, and a rush of warm rough air came over me and then splattered my left cheek, and I opened my eyes in amazement and nearly jumped with excitement.

"If you can understand me, then kiss my right cheek also, OK?"

I closed my eyes again and I was boiling on the inside.

The clammy, heavy-breathed wet patter stuck to the right side of my face this time, and I could not restrain my joy, and my appreciation for "Little Moustache."

"Look, we both have moustaches! We're family. You eat your grass. I eat my vegetables and grains. I'll talk with you."

At that moment, everything else seemed superfluous.

In infinite space and time, we made a connection as two beings. Even though we spoke different languages, and were different species, there was no gap in the communication from one heart to another.

This felt like what life was supposed to be like, fusing our hearts together in this pure mountain air. It was delightful and sincere. Soon it was time to part ways and I said, "I really appreciate your help. Let's close our eyes and give each other our blessings. May you live a happy life and attain a precious human birth in your next life and be drawn to the Dharma."

I closed my eyes and made a wish, while my Brother Antelope also closed his eyes. An antelope and a man had gotten to know each other in a meaningful way.

"What is your blessing?" I asked, with tears in my eyes. I left Brother Antelope, as if saying goodbye to an old friend. "Good brother, the Bodhi road calls us to a long, long journey. My earnest wish is that we both are able to arrive at the same destination."

Every time after contemplating or sharing this story, I am filled with gratitude. My heart is re-inspired to walk the Buddhist path of spiritual awakening, and also to spread the vegan message of revering and respecting all life. This is the essence of the Dharma way. Animals are like humans in the most significant ways and deserve the right to be free and to enjoy life. All living things exist in an interconnected way. In the coexistence between human beings and animals, we are called to try our best to learn how to live in harmony together on this beautiful planet.

My name is Ma Chuo. For many years, I have put my dreams into practice and have travelled the world on foot sharing the Buddhist vegan message. I look forward to a future when every life can have the right to be loved. In this book, the heart-offerings of many Buddhist teachers and practitioners shine light on the connection between the Buddhist Dharma teachings and the vegan path of respecting all life. May your heart be open and may you also be kissed and blessed on both cheeks by the wisdom of the Dharma as I was in the remote Himalayan mountains by "Brother Moustache."

# Contributor Profiles

**Marion Achoulias** is co-initiator of the Montreal March to Close all Slaughterhouses as well as the Meditation at the Vegan Co-op Project, which holds weekly mindfulness sessions for activists. Marion has taught courses in religion, psychology, and ethics at Concordia University, and is an ordained lay student at Blue Cliff Monastery in Upstate New York, a short drive from four local sanctuaries for farmed animals.

**Andrew Bear** is an ordained lay student of Thich Nhat Hanh and chapter leader for the Silicon Valley chapter of Dharma Voices for Animals. Andrew volunteers as a wildlife rehabilitator at the Wildlife Center of Silicon Valley and as a wildlife search and rescue responder with Wildlife Emergency Services.

**David Blatte, J.D.**, served as a public defender in Philadelphia, later had an animal law practice in California, and served as executive director of Vegan Action. A co-founder of Dharma Voices for Animals, David has lived and practiced at Vipassana monasteries in Myanmar and Sri Lanka. A 30-year vegan, he has done over two years of silent intensive Vipassana practice.

**John Bussineau** is author of *The Buddha, The Vegan, and You*. A 20-year member of the Jewel Heart Tibetan Learning Center and student of Gelek Rinpoche, he was named by Rinpoche as Jewel Heart Ambassador for Vegetarianism, Veganism, and Animal Welfare. He has been a chapter leader for the Ann Arbor chapter of Dharma Voices for Animals.

**Dr. Joanne Cacciatore** is a tenured professor at Arizona State University and the founder of the MISS Foundation, an international nonprofit organization with 75 chapters aiding parents whose children have died or are dying. She also started the first therapeutic vegan care-farm, housing 22 animals rescued from abuse. Her research has been published in The Lancet, Death Studies, British Journal of Obstetrics and Gynecology, and Families in Society. Her latest book, *Bearing the Unbearable*, won the 2017 Indies Book of the Year Award in self-help and was included in Oprah's Basket of Favorite Things. Dr. Cacciatore is an ordained Zen priest who stopped eating animals at age 7.

**Ma Chuo**, a calligraphy artist, photographer, free-spirited backpacker, and Buddhist practitioner from Chengdu, China, is over half-way through his ten-year solo walking tour throughout the length and breadth of China, with the aim of spreading the vegan message in every city. So far, Master Ma has received more than 700 car rides while traveling and speaking in over 800 cities and handing out about 150,000 leaflets on veganism and environmental protection. He has been invited to speak at dozens of universities, is vice chair of the World Vegan Organization in China, and vice president of the China Vegetarian Society.

**Alan Dale** is a non-monastic lama in the Kagyu, Nyingma, and Gelug lineages. His teachers have included Chogyam Trungpa Rinpoche, the Dalai Lama, Khensur Rinpoche, Choden Rinpoche, Garchen Rinpoche, and Chetsang Rinpoche. He has been vegetarian and vegan for most of his life. Alan is a digital media expert and CEO of Los Angeles Web Design. He also manages the website VeganBuddhism.com.

**William DiGiorgio** is certified in plant-based nutrition and raw cuisine, and has worked as a vegan chef at several well-known restaurants including Millennium and Living Light. A Vipassana practitioner, he blogs about his vegan lifestyle at VeganDietGuy. com and currently works as a personal chef, caterer, and vegan cooking instructor in Honolulu.

**Tracey Winter Glover, J.D.**, author of Lotus of the Heart: Living Yoga for Personal Wellness and Global Survival, is a former rescue officer with the Humane Society of Huron Valley, MI. After practicing law in Washington, DC, for eight years, she travelled to India to study yoga and meditation. Tracey currently lives in Mobile where she teaches yoga and runs the intersectional animal rights group, "Awakening Respect and Compassion for all Sentient Beings." She is the guardian of 11 rescued cats and two rescued dogs.

**Dr. Jun Gong** is a professor of philosophy at Sun Yat-Sen University in Guangzhou, China, and is director of the Center of Buddhist Studies there. He has been a visiting scholar at Harvard University and is the author of 30 papers and five books on Chinese Buddhism, including *A Study of Humanistic Buddhism*, and is editor of The Chinese Buddhist Review.

**Rev. Heng Sure, Ph.D.**, is the senior monk at the Dharma Realm Buddhist Association. Ordained in 1976 in the Chinese Chan tradition at the City of Ten Thousand Buddhas in Ukiah, California, he made a "three steps, one bow" pilgrimage from South Pasadena to Ukiah for world peace, covering 800 miles over 30 months, while making a full prostration every three steps along the California coast. Rev. Sure writes and performs American Buddhist folk songs (www.dharmaradio.org) and is active in Interfaith dialogue. He spends half of the year in the Queensland bush, conversing with kookaburras.

**Bob Isaacson** is the co-founder and president of Dharma Voices for Animals, an international Buddhist animal advocacy organization. He has practiced the Dharma in the Vipassana tradition for twenty-three years and currently leads two sanghas in the San Diego area, having been trained in Spirit Rock Meditation Center's Community Dharma Leader Program. Bob was a human rights attorney for twenty-five years, specializing in defending people against the death penalty. He presented and won a landmark case before the U.S. Supreme Court when he was 27, the second-youngest attorney in history to appear before the nation's highest court.

**Dr. Joel & Michelle Levey** are authors of several books including *Living in Balance* and *Mindfulness, Meditation, and Mind Fitness*, as well as *The Fine Arts of Relaxation, Concentration, and Meditation*. Founders of Wisdom at Work (www.wisdomatwork.com) as well as All My Relations Sangha and the International Center for Contemplative Inquiry and Research, they are also on the faculty of the University of Minnesota Medical School.

**Sherry Morgado** is a practitioner in the Vietnamese Zen tradition of Thich Nhat Hanh, and has been a vegan since 2007. She lives and practices in Chico, California, where she is active with her sangha and the vegan community, teaching vegan cooking classes and mentoring new vegans. She is also an active member of Dharma Voices for Animals, serving as the U.S Chapter Coordinator and as a member of the Board of Directors.

**Ariel Nessel** is founder of The Pollination Project, providing hundreds of seed grants to community change-makers worldwide. Recent undertakings include hosting meditation retreats for activists, developing solar energy projects, and co-creating a gift-based retreat center. His primary practices are mindfulness, engaged philanthropy, and transformational entrepreneurship.

**Ven. Tashi Nyima** is an ordained monk in the Jonang lineage of Vajrayana (Tibetan) Buddhism, and leads the Universal Compassion Buddhist Congregation, with sanghas in Texas, Mexico, and Argentina. For over 30 years, Lama Tashi has shared the Dharma worldwide in fluent English and Spanish. He has studied under eminent lamas of various lineages, including Tashi Norbu Rinpoche (Jonang), Lama Tsering Ngodup (Kagyu), the Dalai Lama (Geluk), Kenchen Thrangu Rinpoche (Kagyu), Khenchen Tsewang Gyatso Rinpoche (Nyingma), Sakya Trizin Rinpoche (Sakya), and Tashi Gyaltsen Rinpoche (Jonang).

**Dr. Tony Page** published the first major study of Buddhism and animal rights, *Buddhism and Animals: A Buddhist Vision of Humanity's Rightful Relationship with the Animal Kingdom*, and is a full-time lecturer and researcher at Bangkok University, Thailand. He is the author of numerous scholarly papers on English and German literature, as well as on Buddhism, and is also the author of *Vivisection Unveiled: An Exposé of the Medical Futility of Animal Experimentation*.

**Dr. Vicki Seglin** is the co-founder of Fierce Compassion Sangha in Evanston, IL, and is an ordained lay member of Thich Nhat

Hanh's Order of Interbeing. She is the Chicago chapter leader for Dharma Voices for Animals. As a clinical psychologist and educator, she uses mindfulness and compassion practice in her work with clients and students.

**Paul Tarchichi** (Brother Promise) is an ordained monk living in Plum Village, France, in the Vietnamese Zen Buddhist Order of Interbeing founded by Thich Nhat Hanh. A Buddhist monk since 2009, he also has lived and practiced at Thai Plum Village (Thailand) and Blue Cliff Monastery in New York.

**Madeleine Tuttle** is a visionary artist from Switzerland who specializes in painting that celebrates the beauty of animals and nature. She is also a flautist, Waldorf school teacher, long-time vegan cook and coach, gardener, clothing designer, multi-media artisan, and devoted meditator. Her extensive travels on six continents and formal training in Japan in ink brush painting lend a Zen style to her work.

**Dr. Will Tuttle** is author of the best-selling, *The World Peace Diet*, published in 16 languages. A recipient of the Courage of Conscience Award and the Empty Cages Prize, he is also the author of Your Inner Islands and editor of *Circles of Compassion*, as well as the creator of online wellness and advocacy programs. A vegan since 1980 and former Zen monk in the Korean Zen tradition, he is featured in a number of documentary films. A Buddhist practitioner for over 40 years, he is a frequent radio, television, and online presenter, and lectures extensively worldwide.

**Ven. Xianqing** is a Chan (Zen) monk at Beijing Longquan Monastery in Beijing. He is a Dharma lecturer for the monastery's online Buddhist Institute, and is its Director of International Communication. He also holds a doctoral degree in engineering thermophysics. Ven. Xianqing has an extensive interest in and gives lectures on Confucian and Taoist as well as other traditional Chinese cultural classics. He is also Deputy Abbot of Longquan Great Compassion Monastery in the Netherlands.